THE BEFORE HEAVEN I CHING

READING THE TEXT OF CREATION

VOLUME NINE:

RESEARCHES ON THE TOLTEC I CHING

WILLIAM DOUGLAS HORDEN

3 + 4 :: 6 + 1 :: RETURN

Researches on the Toltec I Ching Series:

    Volume One: I Ching Mathematics: The Science of Change

    Volume Two: The Image and Number Treatise: The Oracle and the War on Fate

    Volume Three: The Forest of Fire Pearls Oracle: The Medicine Warrior I Ching

    Volume Four: I Ching Mathematics for the King Wen Version

    Volume Five: Why Study the I Ching? A Brief Course in the Direct Seeing of Reality

    Volume Six: The Open Secret I Ching: The Diviner's Journey and the Road of Freedom

    Volume Seven: The Alchemical I Ching: 64 Keys to the Secret of Internal Transmutation

    Volume Eight: intrachange: I Ching Chess

    Volume Nine: The Before Heaven I Ching: Reading the Text of Creation

Delok Publishing, Ithaca

Copyright © 2019 William Douglas Horden

ISBN: 9781794535985

Dedication

For

999

FOREWORD

My teacher, Master Khigh Alx Diegh, was fond of saying, *The I Ching is the shortest path to fulfilling humanity's two deepest desires—magic and enlightenment.*

The simplicity of consulting the Oracle obscures, for many modern users, the magical elements of the *I Ching*. It seems, after all, that one merely forms a question, casts a few sticks or coins, and looks up the resulting answer in the book. What could be simpler and more straight-forward? And, indeed, what could be less magical?

Yet this description of the ancient ritual of divination barely scratches the surface of the actual act. First of all, the question, or issue of concern, whether spoken aloud or not, is addressed to the *spirit of the I Ching*, the Oracle. The significance of this act cannot be overstated. It means that a modern person, with their rational and religious beliefs in place, sits down and addresses their concerns to a *Spirit*. Secondly, the act of casting yarrow stalks or coins causes the person to slowly and methodically manipulate material objects so as to maximize the opportunity of random chance to determine the outcome—to manipulate, in other words, physical objects for no other reason than the express purpose of being directed by *Spirit* to its reply. And, third, the fact that a person engages in this ritual with the expectation of receiving a meaningful answer means that, at least on an unconscious level, they understand that a *Spirit* is listening to their thoughts, is capable of influencing matter through chance coincidence, and is willing to provide guidance to the living from a perspective of time that includes the future.

From this standpoint, therefore, the act of divination is an ancient practice sharing the same roots of animistic magic as spirit mediumship, shamanism and journeying in the spirit world.

The fact that a modern person can, without the assistance of a specialist-diviner, engage the Oracle on their own, changes nothing of the intrinsic nature of this traditional magic extending back at least three thousand, five hundred years. But it does make it possible for a modern person to step directly onto the path of magic and personally experience, to the degree of their sensitivities, the spirit world. Implicit in this mechanism is the understanding that each encounter with the Oracle increases one's sensitivity to the spirit realm.

Which brings us to Master Khigh's point about the I Ching's path of enlightenment. It is based on the ancient axiom that *the more time one spends with the Oracle, the more one's mind becomes like the Mind of the Oracle.* As the living *Spirit* whose Mind transcends the linear time of past, present and future, spanning the timeless realm of All Creation, the Oracle offers one entry into the nondifferentiated awareness of the enlightened mind. Treating every divination as a sacred ritual of theurgy in which the felt presence of divine *Spirit* manifests within the flux of human affairs, one finds oneself in communion with the One Mind—a communion that brings one's mind into accord with the One, opening the way for the direct transmission of Mind to mind.

It is, of course, my sincere hope that this work might contribute in some small way to your completing your Work in the present lifetime.

3 + 4 :: 6 + 1 :: RETURN

Coatepec
January 2019

INTRODUCTION

This is a book of magic.

Specifically, it is about the true cause of change and, more specifically, how to manifest change within the world of nature and human nature.

These are lessons I learned first-hand from my two lineage-teachers, one a Taoist priest and the other a Rarámuri shaman. In the case of both teachers, I was initiated with the express instruction to make the traditional practices more accessible to the modern mind. Those practices were of a decidedly mystical and ritual nature, impossible to define or reproduce in words, so for the past fifty years I have sought the rational correlates to those teachings in other esoteric disciplines from around the world. It is this grounding of the mystical experience with the rational discipline that gives rise, I believe, to the *law of spiritual cause-and-effect* binding the esoteric traditions into a single, universal practice.

This has led me to believe that ultimately, civilization will be made up of all the best traits and worldviews of all the cultures humanity has produced across the ages. The present book takes a corresponding tack, treating all the spiritual traditions as a single tradition, drawing parallels particularly at those points where the mysticism of the supernatural converges on the rationality of the natural. For this reason, my definition of spiritual traditions has come to include certain worldviews established by early philosophies grappling with the relationship between spirit and nature.

This is not a book of divination.

Specifically, it is not a book about how to use the I Ching or engage the Oracle on the level of divination.[1]

---

[1] These are matters fully articulated in *The Toltec I Ching* and subsequent volumes of *Researches on the Toltec I Ching*, a full listing of which can be found at the back of this book.

It is, rather, an interpretive text of the symbols of the I Ching, which are, in turn, interpretations of the living symbols of Creation. The original indigenous Taoist worldview is one of animism, of nature mysticism, that created symbolic analogs from the archetypal phenomena found in nature.

The diagram below shows the trigrams of the I Ching in the Xiantian, or Fu Xi, arrangement (also called the Earlier Heaven, or Before Heaven, arrangement). This is also known as the Primal Arrangement, since it represents the forces of creation in pre-manifestation equilibrium as they stand before phenomena come into manifestation. By *pre-manifestation equilibrium* is meant that the creative forces are arranged as pairs of opposite-complements that suspend their momentum toward manifestation, preserving their images in the realm of *psyche*: Sun-Moon, Lake-Mountain, Water-Fire, and Lightning-Wind.

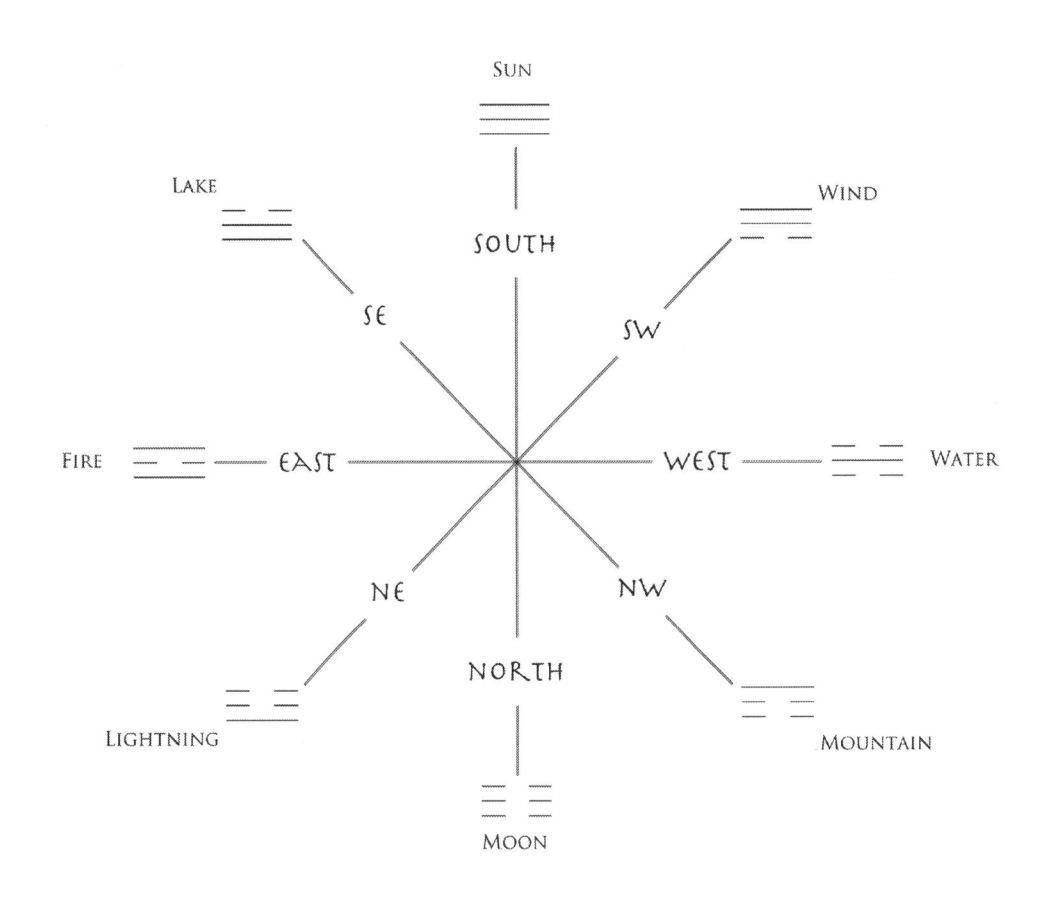

THE BEFORE HEAVEN ARRANGEMENT

This Primal Arrangement is further unpacked as the so-called Order of Completeness, which establishes the natural number, or binary number, sequence. Starting with Sun, the trigrams unfold following the spiral path of completion to Moon: *Sun-Lake-Fire-Lightning-Wind-Water-Mountain-Moon*.

The Order of Completeness

This natural number sequence is the one revealed by Shao Yung around the year 1000. It was later studied by Leibnitz and played a significant role in his discovery of binary mathematics.

THE FU XI, OR BEFORE HEAVEN, SEQUENCE OF HEXAGRAMS

This sequence comprises the text of sixty-four archetypal symbols in their unfolding of Creation-to-Completion (0-to-63).

It is likewise the sequence of symbols used in this book in its *Reading the Text of Creation*. Because it embodies the pre-manifestation stage of change, the primary lens through which it is interpreted is that of, *what kind of actions in the pre-manifestation realm provoke change in the realm of manifestation?* The answer to this question makes up the remainder of this work.

A word about the Line Changes. Because this is not a book about divination, the line changes are not interpreted as transition points between hexagrams. They are, rather, interpreted as the embodiments of *Intent,* compatible with their respective hexagram, *upon which practitioners concentrate their intent as the means by which pre-manifestation images are translated into manifest phenomena.*

The hexagram texts reflect the sequential unfolding of the Underlying Reality of Creation as it stretches across time toward its inevitable Completion. This sequence stands as testament to the remarkable sensitivity of the ancients' intuitive mind, for it not only reflects the unfolding of the macrocosm, but of the microcosm of human nature. This, indeed, is one of their greatest insights, that the symbols of the *I Ching* form the very pattern of perception by which human nature perceives the world—that this pattern is, therefore, embodied in: what is perceived; the perceptions; and, the perceiver.

The lines of the hexagrams are registered as *Intents*. Their texts are short, pointed statements that form the images that practitioners focus their intention on in order to bring their symbolic value into material phenomena in the world of manifestation.

In sum, the hexagrams identify the situation particular to the phase of Creation's unfolding and its characteristic interactions, while the lines point to imagistic *Intents* that make up the magical *practice of manifesting change*. This use of the *I Ching* differs from that of divinatory practice in the world of manifestation in that, divination *reads* the development of change as it extends into the future, whereas concerted concentration of intent on the image-symbols *creates* the development of change as it manifests in the future.

THE BEFORE HEAVEN I CHING

READING THE TEXT OF CREATION

0

CREATION

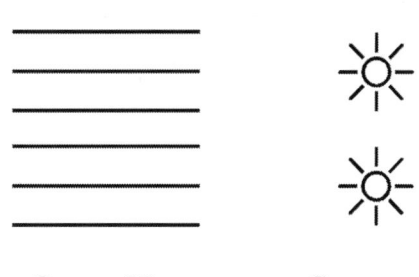

OUTER NATURE:	**SUN**
INNER NATURE:	**SUN**

Sun within, Sun without: Creation within, Creation without

Sun outside symbolizes a new external beginning, while Sun inside symbolizes originality. The seed of potential may fall anywhere, yet it itself is born of the fruit of realization: the cycle of time is without beginning or end—it is like the sky's changing reflection in the timeless ocean's surface. Things are born and die, yet they arise from previous transformation and contribute to successive transformation. Mists coalesce, like spirits gathering, to take on a new fleeting form—the form runs its course and the mists disperse, like spirits returning homeward: every form, no matter how short-lived or long-lived, is a river produced by the confluence of innumerable tributaries of unfathomable intent. Things are born from the unborn, things take form from the formless: that which is unborn cannot die, that which is formless cannot be destroyed. In the endless cycle of transformation, every moment is the confluence of innumerable tributaries of unfathomable intent: every moment is the Act of Creation.

This hexagram is paired with its complement, 63, COMPLETION.

HEXAGRAM SEQUENCE

After things have completed their cycle, they rise again from their ashes:
CREATION is original thought turned back onto itself.

This hexagram speaks to both the universal Act of Creation and the individual act of creation. In both cases, *creation manifests*. The uninitiated perceive only the world of form and so attempt to create in the world of form; they perceive only the world of birth and death and so attempt to create in the world of birth and death. The initiated, however, perceive the world of the formless and so create by coalescing resonant intentions that manifest in the world of form; they perceive the world of the unborn and so create by gathering spiritual allies that manifest in the world of birth and death. The uninitiated attempt to create out of their own power. The initiated create by aligning with the creative power of the universal Act of Creation.

What creates is without an absolute name. It is styled *Tao* by tradition, the universal force that guides everything from within. Though it appears as Intelligence, Mind, Awareness, Essence, Spirit, and Soul, it is *The Way* that gives rise to all of those appearances. This universal *Tao* is mirrored in the microcosmic *tao* of each individual being. It is impossible to engage in individual acts of creation unless one's individual *tao* is aligned with the universal *Tao*. This is the meaning of the ancient wisdom teaching, *All creativity is based on receptivity*—the expression of creative activity, in other words, is wholly dependent on sensitizing oneself to the creative intent of *The Tao*. Such sensitization can only be attained by stilling the unbidden thoughts of the habit mind, thereby opening the way for one's return to original thought. *As Above, So Below*: the birth of the universe is not in any way different than the birth of an original idea.

Original thought has no object upon which it dwells. It produces no image with which it identifies. It is purely the state of being *Tao*. Because original thought does not produce thoughts, nothing obstructs the free, natural and spontaneous *folding back upon itself* that allows for the primordial raw experiencing of the pure state of being *Tao*. This *doubling of awareness* produces neither subject nor object, but an *unconditioned reflection* of pure being, long described in the wisdom teachings as, *Pouring water into water*. When mind perceives mind rather than mind's projections, the conceptual barrier separating universal *Tao* and individual *tao* is ruptured permanently in the state of continuous awakening: the collapse of this barrier initiates a natural, spontaneous and uncontrived momentum whereby the individual *tao* engages in acts of creation that benefit nature, human nature and spirit that are in utter harmony with those of the universal *Tao*.

In the sequence of hexagrams, 0, CREATION follows its complement, 63, COMPLETION. The cycle of creation having run its entire course to completion, it returns to the act of creation in the same way that the seed falls free of the ripened fruit.

MANTIC FORMULA

Returning to the Act of Creation:
You walk among the most ancient gods and goddesses.

Before Heaven means *before manifestation*. This points to the actual *where-ness* in which authentic creation takes place—the realm of *pre-manifestation*. It is the World Soul, the realm of intent that gives rise to the world of manifestation: just as the World Body is the natural environment within which our physical bodies live, the World Soul is the spiritual environment within which our souls live. The uninitiated are aware only of the World Body and so live out their lives attempting to create a lifeway out of their own power within the world of form. The initiated are aware of the World Soul and interact therein with other souls to create the greatest *benefit* for nature, human nature and spirit within the world of manifestation.

The return to the primordial act of creation is possible within the World Soul because of the true nature of time. While time in the manifestation realm is linear, appearing to move from past to future, time in the World Soul is purely cyclical, evoking no sense of development or progress whatsoever. Time is coincident with awareness and the passage of experience—such passage is similar to the cycle of seasons: change occurs but within the same year over and over. This static facet of the World Soul, held in eternal equilibrium, demonstrates the fundamental aspect of the realm of pre-manifestation: *the oneness of time*.

The *origin of the world of manifestation* is what is meant by *the beginning of all things*. This event, the primordial act of creation, cannot be returned to within the linear time of the world of manifestation.

Within the timelessness of the World Soul, however, neither past, present nor future exist: it is a realm of *psyche*, experienced as *psychic substance*, within which all creation arises as intentions that generate images. Because the absence of linear time means that no event is ever lost or forgotten, every event is forever present. To return to the act of creation is to charge one's intent with the image-symbol of the *most ancient souls* conducting the ritual of *the beginning of all things*.

Returning to the Act of Creation signifies one's conscious re-entry into the World Soul, wherein the act of creating the world of manifestation is continuous and never-ending. *You walk among the most ancient gods and goddesses* signifies that one is aware of the other souls within the World Soul and able to recognize those of the greatest creative power. As a whole, this formula signifies that you are able to participate on the most profound levels of co-creation by aligning your reverential intentions with the magnanimous intentions of the all-perfecting souls embodying the living *Tao*.

INTENT

Bottom Line. Radiant lushness: The living world shines from within.

Second Line. Radiant vision: The living eye sees eternity.

Third Line. Radiant heart: The living stone rejoices age after age.

Fourth Line. Radiant memory: The living reincarnation laughs in astonishment.

Fifth Line. Radiant understanding: The living shadow casts a far light.

Top Line. Radiant mind: The living truth speaks its own name.

1

REVELATION

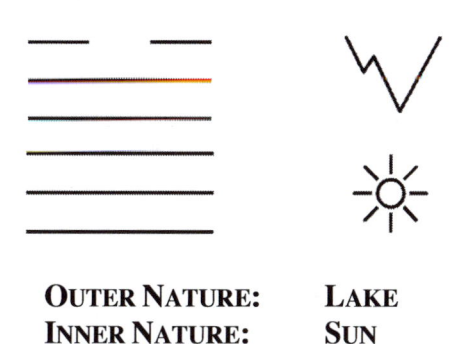

OUTER NATURE: LAKE
INNER NATURE: SUN

Sun within, Lake without: Creation within, Wonder without

Lake outside symbolizes communion with nature and spirit, while Sun inside symbolizes continuing creation. Joy is the natural, spontaneous and uncontrived response to existence. It is the immediate bond between essence and existence, a mutual state of profound communion in which *That which is above* makes itself known to *That which is below*. Communion of such *intimacy* is not constrained to emotions—it is the shared entirety of *memory* and *understanding* that contributes to every soul's most secret intent. This *passing between* souls of esoteric intent is the direct transmission of awareness that transmutes the baser *psychic substance* into its subtle state of continuous awakening. Such is the nature of revelation: *pouring water into water* does not in any way change the essence of the water—but it does magnify its existence. This is because the already-perfected essence of water is the same, but the addition of the *above* into the *below* extends its sphere of awareness into realms of unimagined existence: the essence of awareness may not change but transpersonal *understanding* and *memory* expand the realm of existence of which the soul is aware.

This hexagram is paired with its complement, 62, DISSOLVING.

Hexagram Sequence

After things have arisen, they unveil themselves:
Revelation is the heralding of perfection to come.

Nothing stands closer to Creation than ecstatic reverence. The first and original arisings are images that immediately display themselves as symbols of archetypal meanings. They display themselves not just to one another but to themselves. It is their very mysterious nature as unborn arisings, like waves of the ocean, that charges them with multiple significances of the first order of magnitude: it is their divinity that most exposes their essence and, at the same time, veils their full understanding of the depths of their own mystery. They are themselves the very revelation of Creation, the fount from which all subsequent generations of living symbols flow. They reflect Creation back to Creation and yet turn their back on Creation in order to set in motion the full realization of the purpose of Creation itself. Holding court, gardening, soaring across the sky, chopping wood, carrying water: the most ancient gods and goddesses are always an arm's reach away, forever the very symbols of *innate perfectibility*.

Mantic Formula

Ecstatic communion reveals itself:
You immerse yourself in the oceanic moment.

The infant produces joy for no reason. Ecstasy leaps forward, unbidden, like spontaneous combustion of a fire igniting itself: the innate and quintessential characteristic of the soul, unconditioned joyousness arises spontaneously to reveal the perfecting influence of *original righteousness*. Transcendent delight accompanies the creative soul, who stands forever perched on the edge of the abyss, transfixed witness to the infinitude of mysteries rising from the depths to make their presence known. Within the World Soul, time reveals itself in the spatiality of experience rather than the sequential flow of moments following one another. Outside the flow of temporal experience, the soul experiences the *all-at-once-ness* of the underlying harmony of reality both creating and sustaining the world of appearances. For the initiated, the world of appearances does not veil the underlying reality but, rather, reveals its timeless foundation in the manner in which spirit takes form in nature: the bridge between the World Body and the World Soul lies in the communion of the individual soul and the *spirit of nature*. As a whole, this formula signifies that you are attuned to the most ancient souls and witness to their unfathomable creative intent: such proximity to such beings signifies that one is, oneself, of a more ancient lineage of souls than present *memory* and *understanding* acknowledge.

INTENT

Bottom Line. Transparent fear: All the splinters in the world do not a tree make.

Second Line. Transparent grief: All the mirages in the world do not an oasis make.

Third Line. Transparent aloneness: All the betrayals in the world do not a person make.

Fourth Line. Transparent hope: All the goals in the world do not a purpose make.

Fifth Line. Transparent strength: All the targets in the world do not an arrow make.

Top Line. Transparent faith: All the thunder in the world does not lightning make.

2

FOREKNOWLEDGE

OUTER NATURE: FIRE
INNER NATURE: SUN

Sun within, Fire without: Creation within, Knowledge without

Fire outside symbolizes knowledge, while Sun inside symbolizes creative vision. The shift from *joy* to *knowledge* is a natural one but not always executed gracefully. The *need* to know things in a way that conforms to individual preferences or biases contaminates the meaning and interpretation of the object of knowledge; likewise, the desire to acquire knowledge deemed important by others, especially in relation to motives of self-interest, is traditionally considered *contrived knowledge* and of little intrinsic value. *Deep knowledge*, however, is the upshot of *wonder* and *awe*, the direct result of curiosity and the joy of learning simply by experiencing the new. Knowledge for knowledge's sake is empty, a void of conceptual gymnastics passing itself off as intelligence. The *understanding* that arises from deep knowledge, on the other hand, weaves together all the relationships between things into a tapestry of sacred meaningfulness. Of all the types of knowledge open to the intellect, none is so rare or so valued as true foreknowledge. Of all the types of self-knowledge open to the soul, none is so elusive or so settling as true foreknowledge.

This hexagram is paired with its complement, 61, INTEGRITY.

Hexagram Sequence

After things have revealed their true nature, they illuminate the inevitable:
FOREKNOWLEDGE is mobility within the single eternal moment.

Within the world of manifestation, the arrow of time ensures the unknowability of future events. Within the World Soul, the *oneness of time* makes it possible for souls to encounter constellations of intent that are *both* continually increasing in intensity and coherence *and* absolutely certain to take form in the world of manifestation. The soul filled with wonder and the joy of exploring the whole of the World Soul comes across many groupings of pre-manifestation substance in the far places between the great landmarks and monuments that have long forged the landscape of the world of manifestation. Many of these far-flung groupings of intent lack the intensity and coherence to break through the materialization barrier; of those that do, most constitute short-lived manifestations of a personal or localized nature. But occasionally, diligent wanderers, spurred on by their sense of wonder and insatiable curiosity, follow a track into rich and fertile regions of *psyche* in which large numbers of souls collaborate in erecting a testament to their collective desire. It is these testaments, whether constructive or destructive, that possess the greatest probability of manifestation and, once witnessed, augur the surest sense of that which will inevitably take form in the world of appearances.

Mantic Formula

Seeds sprout and take root underground before they appear:
Your antennas stretch in all directions.

Seeds of intent do not immediately make themselves manifest. They have an organic quality in that they are part of a greater environment and must interact with the other intents around them. All this occurs within the pre-manifestation realm of the World Soul, which is inaccessible to the body's five senses. The soul, however, possesses a wider range of more subtle senses, often likened to the long, flexible antennas of insects able to detect sensations beyond the ken of human senses. That these antennas stretch in all directions means that they reach into the visible and invisible realms both. As a whole, this formula signifies that you discern closely between true foreknowledge and intuitive imagination and, once convinced of a matter's authenticity, you painstakingly determine the most beneficial means and timing of sharing that foreknowledge with others in the world of manifestation.

INTENT

Bottom Line. Timeless harmony: A forest rises anew from the wildfire's ashes.

Second Line. Timeless innocence: The fountain of youth flows anew from every eyeblink.

Third Line. Timeless longing: The eternal flame bursts anew from every moth's resurrection.

Fourth Line. Timeless treasure: The full moon empties anew from awakened memories.

Fifth Line. Timeless light: The shadow of death dies anew from the solar eclipse's passing.

Top Line. Timeless time: The triumph of life revels anew from within the mountain of matter.

3

INTENTION

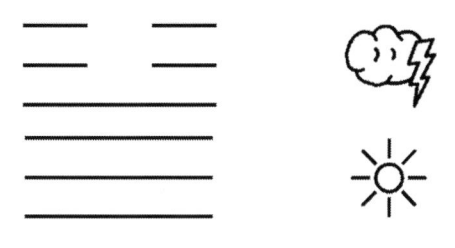

OUTER NATURE: LIGHTNING
INNER NATURE: SUN

Sun within, Lightning without: Creation within, Motivation without

Lightning outside symbolizes inciting events, while Sun inside symbolizes creative power. Desire is not enough. Willfulness is not enough. Aim is not enough. Purpose is not enough. Intention cannot be grasped with words. It is like strength: one can pick up something very heavy or one cannot. Words do not describe the execution of strength. Yet strength can be increased by exertion—exercising strength makes it stronger. One may say that intention is the focusing of attention. But this is merely the crudest of perspectives. Intent is the catalyst of change. It may be like the seed taking root in secret or like the grain of sand being polished by the oyster—or it may be like the lightning bolt falling from a clear sky. What changes thought into intent—and how does focused thought evoke change?

This hexagram is paired with its complement, 60, IDENTIFICATION.

Hexagram Sequence

After things have presaged their destiny, they wish to help build the bridge:
INTENTION is the invisible body working in the invisible realm.

Foreknowledge allows initiates to perceive coming events in the world of manifestation. Where those events are constructive and beneficial for all, they endeavor to help build the bridge between intent in the World Soul and manifestation in the World Body. Where those events are destructive and beneficial only to the shadow-hearted, they endeavor to ruin that bridge before it spans the Two Worlds. The *intentional body,* also called the *dream body,* thus fulfills the initiate's sense of purpose in the invisible realm for the good of the visible realm.

Before awareness bifurcates into the conscious and the unconscious, it is still pure *psyche*. In the world of manifestation, that state of pure *psyche* can only be encountered in dreams. The uninitiated are confused by the dream-state but the initiated are most at home there: they move within the *psychic substance* that *is* the dream-state, in much the same way a fish moves within the ocean. The fish is an intrinsic part of the ocean, just as the ocean *is* all of the animals, plants and elements within its waters. The entire ocean is the dream-state and everything in it is *psychic substance*. The individual awareness within the dream-state encounters other images therein—an animal, a relative, a stone, a cave, and so on—and in those encounters perceives, as if by telepathy, the *intent* each possesses. Intent, then, is *psychic substance* emanating from, and interacting with, *psychic substance*. In this sense, intent is similar to the whale song in that it emanates from the individual and interacts with all those in its surroundings.

Mantic Formula

Forms shift into one another on the way to taking form:
You echo like distant thunder for now.

Psychic substance coalesces into its recognizable form, morphing laboriously as intent consolidates into its final vision. This process mirrors that of thought changing into intent: at first, attention is drawn to something, then thought forms an image of it in reverse in order to grasp its deeper absence, which in turn evokes the *perfecting instinct* of the soul that drives intent.

Intent turned outward changes the relationships between things. Initiates take aim at the relationships in which something is engaged and channel their *psychic substance* into those relationships, finding the places of resonance and dissonance with the *psychic substance* of those bonds. Reinforcing bonds of resonance, improving bonds of dissonance: thought triggers the *perfecting instinct*, which directs intent to work indirectly on changing things by addressing the relationships that sustain them.

Intent turned inward changes states. Intent does not propel the soul on its journeys through the World Soul. Rather, by folding intent back onto itself, the soul undergoes changes of internal state that draw the soul to places in accord with the intent of the World Soul. Not everywhere the soul is called, however, resonates with the soul: it is in this season that the soul first encounters the destructive intentions of the shadow-hearted souls that have surrendered to the counter-Creation.

As a whole, this formula signifies that you are aware of the form into which you are coalescing—just as you are aware that this remains a transitional symbol of your own *perfecting instinct* for the time being.

INTENT

Bottom Line. Absolute focus: Harmonious balance with nature is the priority.

Second Line. Absolute focus: Harmonious cooperation among all people is the priority.

Third Line. Absolute focus: Harmonious acceleration of human potential is the priority.

Fourth Line. Absolute focus: Harmonious equipoise in the midst of upheaval is the priority.

Fifth Line. Absolute focus: Harmonious translation of the angels' message is the priority.

Top Line. Absolute focus: Harmonious traversing of eternity is the priority.

4

RECOGNITION

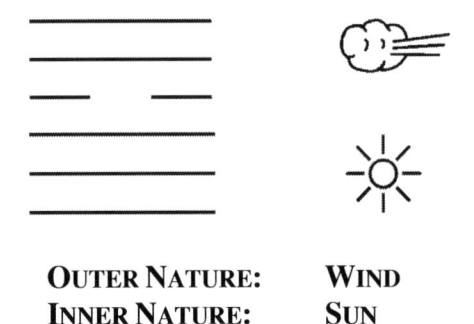

OUTER NATURE:	WIND
INNER NATURE:	SUN

Sun within, Wind without: Creation within, Adaptation without

Wind outside symbolizes adapting to circumstances, while Sun inside symbolizes creative vision. With familiarity and mobility, the soul explores the World Soul with greater confidence and endurance. The ability of the initiated to penetrate ever deeper into the *psychic substance* of the pre-manifestation realm fuels their creative intent: it is, after all, the soul's response to encountering other *intentional bodies* that sets in motion its own participation in the myriad collective efforts to effect life in the world of manifestation.

This hexagram is paired with its complement, 59, INSPIRATION.

Hexagram Sequence

After things have embodied divine volition, they recognize one another:
RECOGNITION is essence welcoming essence.

The highest expression of free will is the voluntary surrender to Divine Will. This surrender is made possible only because the individual intention is attuned to the mystical unity of the underlying harmony beneath the world of appearances. When individual *tao* recognizes itself as the microcosmic reflection of universal *Tao*, the shift from the *becoming of existence* to the *being of essence* is immediate and irreversible: from this transformed perspective, the barrier between subject and object, individual and universal, is dissolved in the mutual identification of essence embracing essence. This transformed perspective simultaneously triggers the *perfecting instinct* within the soul, by which essence is able to recognize the avenues of potential-yet-unrealized within the *existence* of the world of manifestation.

Mantic Formula

The wind carries the sun in its womb:
You return the pearl to the dragon's den.

The emanation of the *One* into the *Many* passes through the World Soul in its descent into the World Body. The return of the *Many* to the *One* likewise passes through the World Soul in its ascent from the World Body. It is the rarest and most sublime form of *recognition* that is capable of discerning those manifestations in the process of returning to the Act of Creation: such sensitivity enables initiates to guide their charge through the World Soul by joining their intentions to theirs in a direct transmission of *memory* and *understanding* between souls.

This season of RECOGNITION carries with it the responsibility of discerning between constructive and destructive endeavors within the World Soul. More than anything, this is a saddening responsibility because the World Soul ought never have become the site of destructive projections aimed at satisfying greed, hatred, violence and domination. Regrettable as this duty is, it is absolutely necessary in order to avoid ever naively aligning with the forces of the counter-Creation.

As a whole, this formula signifies that you possess the refined perceptions of a true initiate and the wisdom to act on them for the benefit of all.

INTENT

Bottom Line. Shadow infant: The sleeping giant awakens.

Second Line. Shadow child: The sleeping ancestor awakens.

Third Line. Shadow youth: The sleeping opposite awakens.

Fourth Line. Shadow adult: The sleeping healer awakens.

Fifth Line. Shadow parent: The sleeping guardian angel awakens.

Top Line. Shadow elder: The sleeping infant awakens.

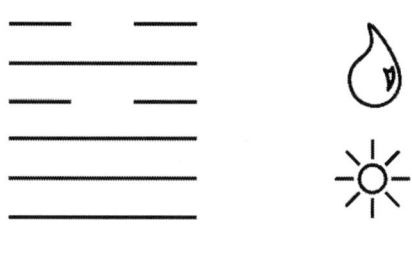

5

INTERPRETATION

OUTER NATURE:	WATER
INNER NATURE:	SUN

Sun within, Water without: Creation within, Mystery without

Water outside symbolizes the Great Mystery, while Sun inside symbolizes the creative drive. Ultimately, nothing lies before awareness other than the Great Mystery. The initiated stand in perpetual awe and astonishment before the monolithic, seamless and omnipresent Living Sphinx of Night: all is ultimately unknowable, a living mystery of infinite potential, every moment an encounter with the Eternal Truth of chaos and cosmos. What extends back before Creation? What extends forward beyond Creation? What are the greater conditions within which all of Creation is held? Without answers to these questions, all knowledge is conditioned by pure sensory experience, whether physical or spiritual—conditioned by the intuitions we receive from pure sensory experience, which stand in place of answers to the fundamental questions. It is these intuitions that color the soul's worldview, determining its personal interpretation of the meaning of existence and the individual's place within it.

This hexagram is paired with its complement, 58, CONFORMITY.

Hexagram Sequence

After things have identified with sameness, they attain true understanding:
INTERPRETATION is the subjective made universal.

Once individual *tao* is aligned with universal *Tao*, understanding penetrates a further veil of the Unknown: the meaning of the Great Mystery is not that it holds a greater secret but that its presence is itself the Truth. This constitutes the Synergistic Horizon, beyond which conscious knowledge cannot reach: *The truth of the Whole cannot be predicted by the truth of the parts.*

Psyche, however, is Truth made manifest—the emanation translating the realm of Pure Thought into the realm of Nature. It is the essence of all things that communes among all things, recognizing the development of each soul and guiding the initiated back through the realm of Pure Thought to The One. *Psyche*, then, is neither conscious nor unconscious—it is the original state of *awareness*, the creative potential to interpret raw awareness into images of meaning: it is the *Imaginal*, the capacity of the creative imagination to interpret the world of unknowable experience into the world of cryptic symbols. This is not simply trading one unknowable for another. Symbols are always cryptic because they each contain a multitude of meanings, but this lack of precision actually enlarges and enriches interpretation by creating a *field of meanings* exponentially greater than any single definition. Interpretation, from this perspective of the manifest realm, is the art of using symbols to express individual experience in such a way as to make it universally meaningful.

From the perspective of the higher emanations, interpretation is the primary act of awareness: every moment is an encounter with the *Text of Creation*, whose angelic language is expressed wholly in the symbols pouring forth from the *One* in its Act of Creation. Interpreting the original divine meaning of symbols is the means by which they are returned to their origin in the *One*. Every act of awareness, then, is an act of interpretation, carrying with it the potential to restore *living symbols* to their eternal meanings.

Mantic Formula

Night and day do not happen at the same time:
You turn the wheel in equal measure.

The symbolic structure of awareness mirrors the symbolic structure of the world of manifestation because both are emanations of the World Soul and its symbolic structure. The alternation of day and night in the manifest world, for example, makes conscious the alternating forces within awareness. The fact that they alternate and do not coincide, beyond transitions of peripheral overlap, establishes a foundational perception and interpretation of change—change in the world of appearances, change in the World Soul, change in the individual soul. The natural alternation of primordial elements that are both opposite and complement signals the need for a harmonious equilibrium in the appreciation of the Creative Duality making up the Great Unity.

Recognition of sameness, though, implies a recognition of difference and it is in this discernment of difference that interpretation plays its crucial role. For the cryptic nature of symbols opens them to misinterpretation, especially when fueled by a soul's greed, hatred, violence and desire for domination. In a self-perpetuating cycle of delusion, such souls invest symbols with their own self-destructive meanings, which in turn are amplified by the multiple meanings inherent to those symbols and thereby reinforce the soul's misinterpretation. War, genocide, racial hatreds, religious enmity, poverty, starvation, lack of potable water, desecration of the environment, unwillingness to cease behaviors destructive to the natural world upon which human survival depends—all these horrors of the world of manifestation are symptoms of the underlying illnesses of intent carried in the depths of eclipsed souls within the World Soul. As a whole, this formula signifies that you do not allow your passion for neutrality and noninterference to deter you from correcting the misinterpretations of symbols within the World Soul in order to alleviate suffering in the World Body.

INTENT

Bottom Line. Golden land: Nature, humanity and the divine blossom together.

Second Line. Golden tears: People separated reunite to blossom together.

Third Line. Golden path: Songs and hearts blossom together.

Fourth Line. Golden sky: Mind and body blossom together.

Fifth Line. Golden star: Heading and destination blossom together.

Top Line. Golden sea: Moon and sun blossom together.

6

CULTIVATION

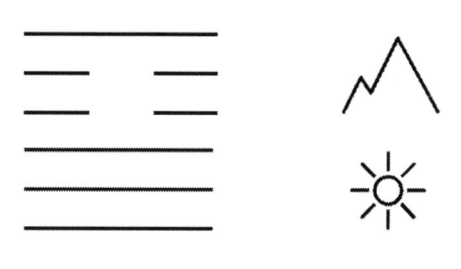

OUTER NATURE:	MOUNTAIN
INNER NATURE:	SUN

Sun within, Mountain without: Creation within, Incubation without

Mountain outside symbolizes tranquil stability, while Sun inside symbolizes ongoing creation. The germ of life grows from within—this is called the ongoing creation of the individual. If this life force is allowed to simply pour out into its environment moment after moment, without being replenished from within, then its life is shortened and its wellbeing diminished. Numerous traditional practices have been handed down from the ancients that check the flow of the life force, keep it more contained within and stabilize its frenetic energies. The same is true on the spiritual level, of course, for the spark of divine fire at the heart of the soul cannot constantly be expended without fortification—here, however, it is the *attention* that must be held in check, returned to its natural state of tranquility and transformed into timelessness. The passage of attention from one thing to another contributes in large part to the experience of time, but it is in the stillness of attention, where awareness dwells complete in the living current of continuing creation, that the threshold of eternity is crossed. And it is here in the World Soul, amid the living exploration of every potential creation, that the initiated turn the *perfecting instinct* onto themselves.

This hexagram is paired with its complement, 57, CONSECRATION.

Hexagram Sequence

After things have expressed true being, they refine their becoming:
Cultivation is the practice of perfecting.

In the face of the Great Mystery, the soul's spontaneous expression of its own symbolic nature reveals its potential state of transmutation from *becoming* into *being*. This encounter with the Living Sphinx of Night makes apparent the soul's relationship with the wisdom teachings: the ongoing light-giving creation of the world of manifestation is utterly dependent on the unchanging night-embracing void of the pre-manifestation world. The initiated glimpse their innate perfectibility in the mirror of the void and perceive, beyond all doubt, the road forward to that inevitability—the road of inner cultivation leading to realization of potential. Once utilized in the practice of self-liberation, the wisdom teachings make themselves available for the cultivation of others' garden of becoming.

Mantic Formula

Dark is merely the absence of light:
You illuminate the heart of the mountain.

There exists a kind of *spiritual darkness* that has nothing to do with the Living Sphinx of Night or any of the myriad symbols of the Divine Feminine that is both womb and midwife of all creation. *Spiritual darkness* is the nihilism that neither produces nor sustains; it is merely the absence of the One Light, whose radiance emanates throughout Creation. It requires nothing, in other words, to produce *spiritual darkness* except for the absence of *spiritual light*. It requires spiritual practice, handed down as wisdom teachings from the ancients, however, to produce *spiritual light*: such cultivation takes place both in the World Soul and the world of manifestation—it is the embodiment of the soul's path, certainly, that imbues the initiated with the *spiritual light* to guide others through the *spiritual darkness*. As a whole, this formula signifies that you penetrate into the very depths of the material world in search of opportunities to convert the cave of nihilism into the secret garden of life-giving rainclouds.

INTENT

Bottom Line. Sincere air: Antenna sprout from the forehead to touch everything at once.

Second Line. Sincere fire: Cities of crystal arise everywhere at once.

Third Line. Sincere water: Jade rivers overflow everywhere at once.

Fourth Line. Sincere light: Angelic wings sprout from behind to embrace everything at once.

Fifth Line. Sincere ether: Invisible gods and goddesses return everywhere at once.

Top Line. Sincere earth: An obsidian mirror reflects everything at once.

7

ORIENTATION

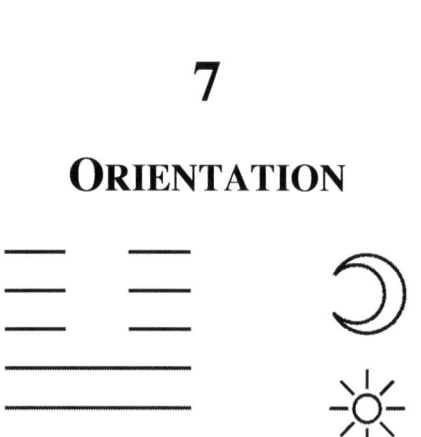

OUTER NATURE: MOON
INNER NATURE: SUN

Sun within, Moon without: Creation within, Completion without

Moon outside symbolizes completion of a cycle, while Sun inside symbolizes beginning of a cycle. Once firmly established, the unfolding of Creation enters the phase of founding a new World Age. There are few times more disorienting than those transitions between the old order and the new. Roles and relationships are turned upside-down and alliances shift without warning. It is the beginning of a new era but not everyone is willing to let the old era pass away. As constructive a time it is for the vanguard of change, it is an equally destructive time for the rearguard of the status quo. This is the time of the *Great Pivot*, the renewal of *spiritual light* as *The Springtide* of the World Soul casts the counter-spell banishing *spiritual darkness*. The uninitiated flail about in the uncertainty of the world of appearances, while the initiated join their intents to bring a new equilibrium to the realm of the *underlying harmony*.

This hexagram is paired with its complement, 56, RECAPITULATION.

Hexagram Sequence

After things have taken up self-discipline, they explore every realm:
Orientation is the inner compass.

The wisdom teachings of the ancients provide the initiated with a center of awareness that is coincident with *The Center* of all Creation. In this sense, the initiated *are* the World Axis joining *That Which Is Above* with *That Which Is Below*. Wherever such a soul stands *is* the center of the world. Like the eye of a hurricane, the initiated stand still in the timeless center of the raging storm of time. All change moves around such individuals, all experience passes through them: there is nowhere to go, there is nowhere to return. All the realms of Creation mirror the soul whose intent is forged lightning and whose vessel sails the sea of spirit. In the cosmic twilight of the gods, as the era of night reverses its path back to the era of light, those who have joined together to channel their intents into creating and sustaining the horrors of the world of manifestation find themselves subsumed by the very *spiritual darkness* they had summoned for so many generations of human nature. The initiated are natural explorers, seeking to know firsthand every region of the World Soul, intending every blossom of *psychic substance* to enrich the lushness and diversity of the ever-perfecting world of manifestation. As the Winter Solstice pivots the year well ahead of Spring, the current phase of Creation initiates the coming World Age of Light.

Mantic Formula

No time is lost between lives:
Across the arc of lives, you do not lose the Way.

Centuries may pass between incarnations but for the soul, it is as if not a moment passed. That which abides in the timeless does not know time, any more than that which abides in time can know the timeless. For the uninitiated, who lack the good fortune to be exposed to the ancients' wisdom teachings, the realm of time is a whirlwind of sensations that veils the soul's memory of the timeless realm. For the initiated, however, the realm of time is a moving manifestation of the still point of the timeless realm—it does not veil the underlying reality because the soul, trained in the mysteries of Creation, never cuts its umbilical cord to the World Soul. As a whole, this formula signifies that you keep your bearings across all your incarnations because *That Which Is Below is the same* as *That Which Is Above*—because your individual *tao* is the conscious manifestation of the universal *Tao*.

INTENT

Bottom Line. True calling: Nature mysticism sets the course of destiny.

Second Line. True impartiality: The extremes cannot set the course of destiny.

Third Line. True conversion: Self-sacrifice sets the course of destiny.

Fourth Line. True freedom: Mastering focus sets the course of destiny.

Fifth Line. True art: Materialism cannot set the course of destiny.

Top Line. True discipline: Personal realization sets the course of destiny.

8
DEVOTION

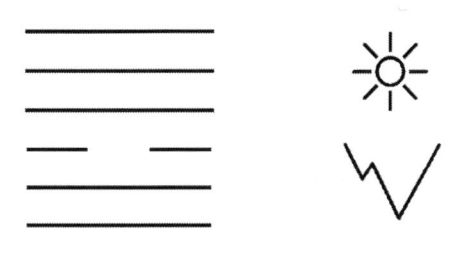

OUTER NATURE: SUN
INNER NATURE: LAKE

Lake within, Sun without: Wonder within, Creation without

Sun outside symbolizes a new beginning, while Lake inside symbolizes communion. A new era brings high spirits, the hopes for a break from the regrets of the past and a fulfillment of the promises of the future. Devotion to the change is nearly absolute and care must be taken that innocents do not fall into zealotry. This destructive nature of devotion has long been a concern of initiates, who find that the uninitiated fixate their positive affections on the baser aspects of the object of their devotion—this paradox extends even into spirituality, where the shadow of religious intolerance and hatred fuels the multi-generational manifestation of zealotry in the world of appearances. True devotion, of course, originates in the World Soul, where it first overwhelms the soul as the floodtide of *Love Of Creation*. All love, indeed, can be seen as originally arising from the spiritual devotion that souls radiate in their encounter with the glory and majesty of Creation. It is particularly from this perspective that the initiated respond to the new era with a kind of recapitulation of that primordial devotion.

This hexagram is paired with its complement, 55, RELAXATION.

HEXAGRAM SEQUENCE

After things have found their bearings, they hold fast to the path:
DEVOTION is the sunflower facing the sun.

Devotion is of two types: *living devotion* and *dead devotion*. Living devotion is the unswerving embrace of faithfulness and steadfast dedication to a spirit, soul or body that is a living presence in one's life. Dead devotion, on the other hand, is loyalty and commitment to a spirit, soul or body that is no longer a living presence in one's life. The issue here is presence—for *spirit, soul or body* plainly refers to the *idea* or *ideal* to which one devotes oneself. Dead devotion is a particular problem in the world of manifestation, for the habit mind of human nature does not relinquish its belief in the worthiness of what it has devoted itself to—when something of past worthiness is no longer worthy of devotion, in other words, the habit mind prefers to maintain its commitment rather than admit to itself that it is wrong to so continue. Living devotion, though, maintains constancy only in the face of the continuing presence of worthiness—if the *righteous energy* departs its vessel, then the initiated withdraw their dedication, for the very root of intent draws sustenance from the primordial ground of devotion. That to which the initiated are devoted embodies the abiding traits of holiness, sanctity, wholeness and loving-kindness: it is what ennobles the soul, enriches the mind, inspires the heart and gladdens the body. There is, plainly, no higher wisdom than loving *that which is greater than oneself* and devoting one's highest intent to nurturing its wellbeing in the world of manifestation.

MANTIC FORMULA

The inner compass points true to the lodestar:
Your heart points true to the One.

In communion with the *One*, the soul enters into the *ecstatic moment* of the Act of Creation, which opens the pathways to authentic communion with all other souls—these pathways establish the mutual opening of *memory* and *understanding* with all other souls, whether mineral, vegetable, animal or spirit. The *One* is ever the lodestar, the Source of all Creation, the fount of Love and Adoration the initiated share. So sublime the devotion expressed by the initiated both within the World Soul and World Body, that they embody the very act of *Uniting Opposites* in a perfect mirroring of the *One* in its continuing spontaneous outpouring of *Universal Benefit*. All of nature rejoices every dawn, all of spirit worships the *One Light*: there is no greater magic than to be welcomed into the *mind of heaven*. As a whole, this formula signifies that you follow the path of *living devotion*, your heart filled with the awe and devoutness that is the hallmark of a soul whose quest for the never-changing sacred has been fulfilled.

INTENT

Bottom Line. Whole-hearted trust: Patience in the face of complexity is not a weakness.

Second Line. Whole-hearted trust: The well-planted tree grows to cover the world with its branches.

Third Line. Whole-hearted trust: The guardian angel forever abides in the primordial home.

Fourth Line. Whole-hearted trust: Betrayal stirs faith in a higher order of love.

Fifth Line. Whole-hearted trust: The mystic burns with the yearning of ten thousand lifetimes.

Top Line. Whole-hearted trust: After waking, the monk disappears in the mountaintops.

9

IMMERSION

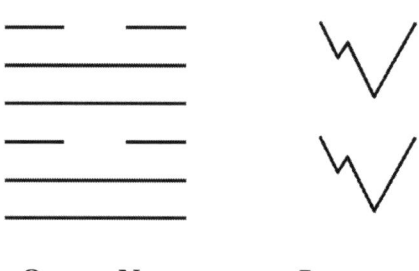

OUTER NATURE:	LAKE
INNER NATURE:	LAKE

Lake within, Lake without: Wonder within, Wonder without

Lake outside symbolizes mystical communion between nature and human nature, while Lake inside symbolizes mystical communion between the divine and human nature. The ecstatic life is the living gift of the ancient gods and goddesses. This is the natural state of human nature, as evidenced by the newborn's blinding euphoria. It requires no new knowledge or experience to achieve this state, merely conscious self-remembering of one's emergence into the world of manifestation. Yet, it is a state that proves to be most elusive for the vast majority of people—there exist so many reasoned justifications for despair that even well-intentioned folks cannot conceive of transcending the grief, horror and suffering so prevalent in daily life. However, this is just the reason the soul enters into the world of manifestation: to incorporate the fully-human experience of mortality into the *memory* and *understanding* of the immortal soul—and, to contribute to the eventual transcendence of all suffering within the world of manifestation. The initiated incorporate the ancients' wisdom teachings and so act on the knowledge that their own physical manifestation within the World Body is itself the materialization of their soul's intent within the World Soul.

This hexagram is paired with its complement, 54, EXTINGUISHING.

Hexagram Sequence

After things have dedicated their lifetime, they dwell in the mystic:
IMMERSION is the water drop returned to the ocean.

Devoting this incarnation to *The Benefit Of All*, the initiated find it increasingly difficult to treat the manifestation realm differently than the pre-manifestation realm. The single-minded concentration on the immortal's intentionality manifests in the mortal's concurrent worldview, attitude and behavior—one's *deep participation*, one's complete immersion, in the world of manifestation, especially in the world of nature comes to mirror one's *deep participation* in the pre-manifestation world of *psyche*. One of the long-held secrets of the ancients, still handed down to their descendants in indigenous communities, is their use of the World Soul as their concurrent homeland, a place where their souls may dwell in peace and in the lifeway they adore: this is the domain of their immortal souls, a refuge from the industrialization of civilization and its turning away from primary nature. The uninitiated lack recourse to the spirit world and so are overwhelmed by the world's suffering. The *perfecting instinct* of the initiated, though, brings their attention to white-hot focus on the *underlying perfection* of all manifestation—a view in perfect accord with their souls' experience in the pre-manifestation realm of the World Soul. *Deep participation* in the *innate perfectibility* of the World Body gains the initiated entry into ecstatic communion with the *One*, the natural and spontaneous consequence of returning elements of the *Many* back to the *One*.

Mantic Formula

The body is a reward for self-sacrifice:
You are the source and destination of all wonder.

Plants do not know they are going to die. Animals do not know they are going to die. Angels cannot die. Gods and goddesses cannot die. Human beings alone know they are going to die. The decision of the soul to enter into the mortal body and experience the full range of mortal conditions is universally honored as a most noble and exalted act of self-sacrifice. In recompense, all the delights and joys of the body are open to experience, as well. The heights of such delights bring the mortal face-to-face with the ecstatic immortal—an encounter closing all distance between the two by erasing all from awareness but the present eternal moment of ecstatic perfection. It is in this encounter that the mortal self ceases to identify with its mortality and identifies wholly with the immortal soul—even as the soul ceases to identify with its sense of individuality and identifies wholly with the *One Mind*. As a whole, this formula signifies that you are welcomed into the *mind of heaven*, where, in *deep participation* with the coming-and-going of souls, you witness the ecstatic union binding All in the ongoing act of underlying communion that makes of all worlds the *secret homeland*.

INTENT

Bottom Line. Stopping progress: The nature mystic is content with contentment.

Second Line. Stopping desecration: The bottomless hole is finally filled.

Third Line. Stopping self-importance: The anonymous wanderer swallows the sea in a single gulp.

Fourth Line. Stopping encapsulation: The healer breaks through the barrier of knowledge.

Fifth Line. Stopping time: The nomad abides in no dwelling place.

Top Line. Stopping mind: The practice becomes the lifeway.

10

PASSION

OUTER NATURE: FIRE
INNER NATURE: LAKE

Lake within, Fire without: Wonder within, Knowledge without

Fire outside symbolizes learning about nature, while Lake inside symbolizes the mystical experience. To learn about nature is to step into the footprints of the ancients, who experienced all of nature as spirit. Such perception arises from the recognition that one has a visible half and an invisible half—and that one is not alone in that state of being, but that everything in nature likewise has a visible half and an invisible half. The ancients called the visible half *body* and the invisible half *spirit*. Just as a person lifting a rock was acting body-to-body with the rock, a person carving a rock into a talisman in order to release its spirit into the world was acting spirit-to-spirit with the soul of the rock. The universal invisible half of all things, in other words, they called spirit but the individualized spirit taking on an identity they called soul—just as they perceived the whole of the sea to be called spirit and each of its individual waves to be called soul. For the ancients, it was a measure of disrespect and irreverence to act solely body-to-body; for this reason, they established rituals and lifeways of *mystical passion* that ensured their every act was simultaneously one of spirit-to-spirit. This passion has always been thought of as the *love of life* unifying opposites.

This hexagram is paired with its complement, 53, DISILLUSIONING.

Hexagram Sequence

After things have immersed themselves in awe, they soar into the heavens:
Passion is the ecstatic life.

Immersion in Creation engenders the most profound state of awe—the initiated train to not let the moment pass right away, but to stop it in its tracks so that they might abide within its oceanic ebb and flow of reverence and wonder: by extending the moment longer and longer, by expanding the center wider and wider, the initiated allow the explosion of awe to sustain itself indefinitely, building momentum that lifts them into reunion with the *One*. Prolonging this moment, building this momentum, transforms the spark of awe into the sustained bonfire of *mystical passion*. This form of sustained passion is the underlying communion among all beings that opens the soul's pathway to the *ecstatic life*. And it is this form of sustained passion that fuels the soul's intent and attracts spiritual allies dedicated to the same overarching purpose, *To Benefit All*.

Mantic Formula

The soul draws the body closer:
You find the spirit of nature living in your own house.

The delights of the body mimic the delights of the soul. Uplifted into the presence of the Divine, the soul is released from all sense of homesickness or amnesia: no thought invades the inner sanctum of sacred exultation, the high bliss of Universal Communion drawing all of *That Which Is Below* up into the welcoming embrace of *That Which Is Above*. The delights of the soul mimic the butterfly, the embodiment of that which lives solely on the nectar of beauty; the delights of the body mimic the angel, the transmutation of that which strives to return to the Divine. There is no end to the paths of passion in the world of manifestation, one for every individual seeking the transcendent road of realized potential. As a whole, this formula signifies that you follow your passion to glory.

INTENT

Bottom Line. Stirring space: No possibility too extraordinary to emerge.

Second Line. Stirring history: Generations pass in heroic self-sacrifice.

Third Line. Stirring moonlight: The ancient thief masters the invisibility spell.

Fourth Line. Stirring opposite: The sword of peace ever sheathed.

Fifth Line. Stirring heart: Swans mate for life in the bonfire of ice.

Top Line. Stirring sight: The mystic becomes the prophet when lightning strikes the inner void.

11

Projection

Outer Nature: Lightning
Inner Nature: Lake

Lake within, Lightning without: Wonder within, Motivation without

Lightning outside symbolizes inspiration, while Lake inside symbolizes communion with the invisible. Those who are impassioned inspire others; those who are enthusiastic lift the spirits of others. Such people clearly see something that others want to see, feel something others want to feel. People place their faith in such a one, grateful to have found someone whose vision resonates with their own deeper hopes, dreams and feelings. Grave responsibilities accompany such visionaries, for to betray the faith of innocents upsets the equilibrium a hundredfold more than ordinary failure of intent. Nonetheless, true visionaries persist—not because they seek followers or fame, but because they are called to visualize the emerging materialization ahead of others in order to help crystalize its fullest realization.

This hexagram is paired with its complement, 52, Autonomy.

HEXAGRAM SEQUENCE

After things have tasted bliss, they seek to extend wellbeing:
PROJECTION is casting forward the vision.

The uninitiated seek to see the future from their standpoint within the world of manifestation; try as they might, the linear nature of time within the world of appearances does not permit them an authentic view beyond the present moment of awareness. The initiated establish their standpoint in the realm of pre-manifestation, where the archetypal forms exist in all their grandeur; the cyclic nature of time in the World Soul permits them to observe the archetypal forms shape-shifting as their *psychic substance* evolves into their intended embodiment. What makes the visionary's art more specialized lies in their capacity to maintain their standpoint within the World Soul even as they project their awareness forward within the world of manifestation—by synchronizing, in other words, the linear time of manifestation and the cyclic time of pre-manifestation in order to see ahead the time, place and intensity of a specific change's manifestation. While unique, the visionary's art is a specialized adaptation of the initiated souls' resolve to abide in both the realm of matter and the realm of *psyche* concurrently.

MANTIC FORMULA

One hundred generations of the Golden Age of Peace and Prospering:
You become the inevitable.

Visionaries are often cast as either *prophets of doom* or *prophets of light*. Among the uninitiated seeking attention, it is generally assumed more advantageous to predict doom, since the ways of human nature tend to produce more catastrophes than blessings; the few choosing to predict constructive futures do so either to stand out from the others or out of a naïve hope born of their individual ordeals. Among the initiated, however, visionaries do not strive for visions—rather, there is something about the momentum building toward a particular manifestation that calls the visionary's attention. Since the ancients' time, great visionaries have pointed to an earth-shaking transformation, a Golden Age that will last thousands of years: though they have not specified its exact arrival, it is widely-acknowledged that its time is near. As a whole, this formula signifies that you can see parts of the Great Transformation emerging as the present era ends—and that you so closely identify with helping materialize the coming Golden Age that you become part of its inevitability.

INTENT

Bottom Line. Shattering dominion: The only way forward is back to the old ways.

Second Line. Shattering domestication: Dogs everywhere reclaim their wolf nature.

Third Line. Shattering distraction: Without a continual flame the water fails to boil.

Fourth Line. Shattering illusion: The self inevitably arrives at the last mask.

Fifth Line. Shattering authority: The sun shines on all equally.

Top Line. Shattering dogma: The god of rain does not come begging for a drink of water.

12

DUALITY

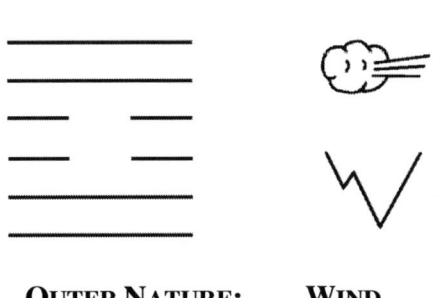

OUTER NATURE:	**WIND**
INNER NATURE:	**LAKE**

Lake within, Wind without: Wonder within, Adaptation without

Wind outside symbolizes patient resolution, while Lake inside symbolizes open-hearted appreciation. Those who consciously abide in both realms concurrently learn the secret art of harmonizing the *Great Duality* that dwells at the heart of everything. Since ancient times, the creative forces making up the *Great Duality* have been called *Yang* and *Yin*. *Yang* is thought of as *Direct Purposeful Action,* while *Yin* is thought of as *Nurturing Without Striving*. Both halves are always present within an entity but only one is leading at a time, just as there is always light and dark but it is never day and night in the same place at the same time. When *True Yang* leads, it is like tunneling through a mountain to reach the sea. When *True Yin* leads, it is like a river going around the mountain to reach the sea—only the river is not striving to reach the sea: it is simply watering everything it touches on its course. *False Yang* arises when it tries to tunnel through an iron mountain—irritation quickly escalates to frustration, anger, hostility and aggression. *False Yin* arises when the river dries up because it is no longer renewed by waters from above—resentment quickly escalates to self-pity, hopelessness, apathy and depression. *False Yang* does not improve by continuing to tunnel through iron, *False Yin* does not improve by continuing to nurture when it has nothing left to give. The secret of harmonizing the creative duality is straight-forward: *False Yang* must be treated with *True Yin,* while *False Yin* must be treated with *True Yang*. When *Direct Purposeful Action* runs its course and becomes self-defeating, then one must turn to the kind of selfless service epitomized by *Nurturing Without Striving*. Likewise, when *Nurturing Without Striving* has run its course and becomes self-defeating, then one must turn to the kind of energetic activity epitomized by

Direct Purposeful Action. Identifying one's creative halves and being able to shift back and forth between them has long been considered essential to the training of the initiated body.

This hexagram is paired with its complement, 51, CONCENTRATION.

HEXAGRAM SEQUENCE

After things have plumbed the well of time, they discover the root of the World Tree:
DUALITY is the firstborn of Creation.

Original Duality arises at the moment of the primordial Act of Creation, as intrinsic to the Beginning as the *One* itself. Its first manifestation lies in the polarity between Being and Nonbeing. One view of the ancients is that this duality exists *prior* to the primordial Act of Creation, in the sense that Being arises from the unexpressed, unmanifested potential of Nonbeing—that the whole of Creation-Being cannot arise out of *nothing* but, rather, from a Nonmanifest-Nonbeing, which, contrary to *nothing*, has actual existence. A second view is that the *One* precedes the primordial Act of Creation and that its intrinsic nature is *unborn, uncreated*, and so has always existed—from this perspective, the *One* creates Nonbeing alongside Being as the mechanism to ensure the *continuing creation* of All Things: such a mechanism utilizes the unexpressed, unmanifested potential of Nonbeing as the well of infinite possibilities from which to draw in its continuing act of creating Being. A third view of the ancients is based upon the dictum, *That which is Above is the Same as That which is Below*, by which a thoughtful examination of the microcosm might produce a meaningful interpretation of the macrocosm: this view holds that the unborn eternal *One* is actually and fundamentally comprised of the *Great Duality*, the two Creative Forces whose *mystical union*, based on mutual attraction and interpenetration, produces a child, the whole of Creation.

According to tradition, the root of the World Tree is in the underworld, where most of the uninitiated dwell, having not yet climbed to the middle level of the world of manifestation.

Mantic Formula

The Morning Star and Evening Star are both Venus:
You are your twin.

The *Great Duality* is difficult to distinguish from the *Great Unity*. Their appearances, so dissimilar at first, constantly shift into one another upon closer inspection. One reason for this is that the Unity has no absolute characteristics, while the Duality has an infinitude. Nothing can be said in description of the *One*, except that it is unconditioned, so to do so would condition and limit it. Of the *Two*, however, we can see its shadow cast everywhere—light and dark, day and night, positive and negative, hot and cold, dry and wet, up and down, back and forward, early and late, before and after, young and old, right and left, conservative and progressive, conscious and unconscious, movement and stillness, yang and yin, and so on: an infinite list of opposite-complements that make up their respective wholes. This fundamental truth of the archetypal nature of Creation is meaningless unless applied to oneself: *Everything contains its own contradiction*. As a whole, this formula signifies that you recognize your reflection in the *mirror of eternity*—that you are able to identify your creative halves and consciously shift between them in response to the needs of circumstances.

Intent

Bottom Line. Balanced reaction: Immediate adaptations to human actions.

Second Line. Balanced conscience: Wrongs forgiven and rights restored.

Third Line. Balanced gaze: Both paths lead to the goal.

Fourth Line. Balanced belief: Angels have no religion.

Fifth Line. Balanced endurance: Savants pivot from the middle.

Top Line. Balanced scale: The river flows from an inexhaustible source.

13

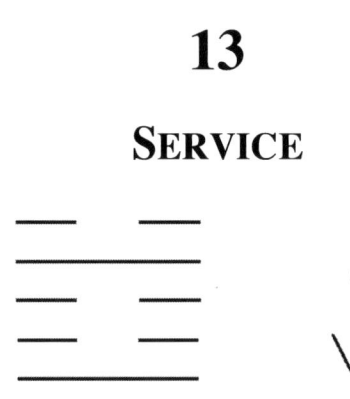

SERVICE

OUTER NATURE: WATER
INNER NATURE: LAKE

Lake within, Water without: Wonder within, Mystery without

Water outside symbolizes the Great Mystery, while Lake inside symbolizes joyous abandon. *True Yin* is that which *Nurtures Without Striving*—it longs to be of service to all beings because of its *love of life*. In this sense, *life* is represented by Water, the symbol of the Great Mystery, the Unknown, the Deep: no matter how far we penetrate into the mysteries of life, new horizons ever present even greater mysteries: *mystery* is the principle foremost characteristic of *life*, especially in regard to the unfathomability of human nature. Similarly, *love* is represented by Lake, the symbol of joy, communion, affection, appreciation, carefree abandon: the natural and spontaneous response to existence is *ecstasy*, the birthright bestowed upon every individual at infancy. *True Yin* views the entire panoply of *life* as the mystifying *field of perfecting*, the unconditioned *love* of which evokes one's *perfecting instinct*: it is in this way that one spontaneously responds to others' evolution, joyously contributing to their advance by serving their soul's true needs. In this sense, *service* is the well of happiness overflowing into the lives of others.

This hexagram is paired with its complement, 50, RECOLLECTION.

Hexagram Sequence

After things have doubled within, they double without:
SERVICE is benefitting all at the same time.

Harmonizing one's own duality naturally turns outward, seeing others as one's other half in a similar act of harmonizing duality by balancing deficiency and excess wherever they present themselves. *False Yang* is known as *excess yang*, which must be balanced with *True Yin*. *False Yin* is known as *yin deficiency*, which must be balanced with *True Yang*. Therefore: sometimes one balances using *Nurturing Without Striving* and other times one balances using *Direct Purposeful Action*. The mechanism of harmonizing dualities is a matter of knowledge and intuition; the reason for serving others is *love*. The sun shines on everything equally, rain falls on everything equally, soil sustains everything equally: *Universal Love* holds nothing back, favors nothing—such is the model that the initiated follow. No one is ever fully initiated until they selflessly and joyously serve All equally.

Mantic Formula

The soul draws others closer:
You find the wellspring of generosity within you.

The highest ethical value is that of self-sacrifice. Seeing others as yourself, seeing yourself as others—eliminating self-importance, serving the best interests of others: if one is unable to do this, how will one commune with the *One*, sacrifice willingly for the *One*, dissolve ecstatically into the *One*? For the uninitiated, service is the lowest rung of status; for the initiated, the highest. Within the World Soul of pre-manifestation, the initiated sit beside the *well of benefit*, offering all who pass a drink. As a whole, this formula signifies that you possess the generosity of spirit shared by all great-souled ones.

INTENT

Bottom Line. Tempered imbalance: Whole and part benefit one another.

Second Line. Tempered vindication: Healing old wounds avoids them re-opening.

Third Line. Tempered preconceptions: Reading the minds of the ancients echoes their teachings.

Fourth Line. Tempered restlessness: Forgetting self in the midst of the ecstatic life.

Fifth Line. Tempered identity: The benefactor is transformed in the gift.

Top Line. Tempered cynicism: The whole seeks the best for all.

14

STEEPING

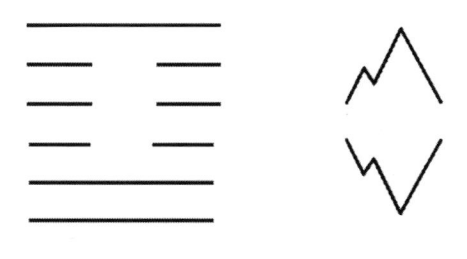

OUTER NATURE: MOUNTAIN
INNER NATURE: LAKE

Lake within, Mountain without: Wonder within, Incubation without

Mountain outside symbolizes restraint, while Lake inside symbolizes enthusiasm. Taking up a course of action, especially one of service, achieves little unless it is engaged in for a prolonged period of time. This is so because the skills to be of service are as much attitudinal as physical—it takes time and practice and, above all, sincerity, to truly be of use to others. However, because this is part of one's self-realization practice, it should not pass unnoticed that this period of time is serving one, as well: tea steeps until it has fully infused the water, service steeps until it fully infuses the soul. The initiated settle into a long-range project, mastering the skills involved even as they are transformed and refined through this course of action. This hexagram shows internal enthusiasm and excitement being held in check by external circumstances—there is nowhere to go, no advance: settling in to a constructive course of action, maintaining one's enthusiasm day after day, refraining from looking ahead for progress or advance—such is the measure of one's patient performance of the practice.

This hexagram is paired with its complement, 49, COMMUNION.

Hexagram Sequence

After things have elevated others, they tread the timeless:
Steeping is dwelling in interpenetration.

Tea changes the water, water changes the tea: they interpenetrate, which is the secret mechanism by which the mystical marriage of reality and the world of appearances is achieved. The statue of the golden lion is traditionally offered up as an example, for the lion has no substance without the gold, any more than the gold has any form without the lion: the gold and the lion interpenetrate perfectly, just as the substance of reality and the form of appearances interpenetrate completely—neither would exist without the other. In true service, the line between self and other blurs dramatically and, indeed, in the steeping of high service, disappears completely. Placing others above oneself in this manner opens the gate to the timeless realm of *psychic substance*, wherein ever deeper levels of service reveal themselves. As the soul steeps in the *psychic substance* of the World Soul, it finds itself in interpenetration with that *psychic substance*, unable to maintain the line between self and *psychic substance*. At one with the *psychic substance*, the soul's intent is at one with the intent of the World Soul, facilitating the marshaling of beneficial *psychic substance* into places of greatest need.

Mantic Formula

A mountain reflected in a lake:
You pass ten thousand lifetimes in awe.

At one with the *One*, the initiated rest in tranquil equipoise at the Center, regardless where they are, whether standing, sitting, walking or lying down. At one with the *One*, the initiated dwell in peace and contentment at the Center, regardless where they are, whether embroiled in activity or deep asleep. At one with the *One*, the initiated listen to the celestial heartbeat at the Center, regardless where they are, whether teaching, studying or meditating. At one with the *One*: the Center is everywhere, the *secret garden* of peaceful bliss wherein the soul is permeated by the presence of the ancient gods and goddesses continuing the Act of Creation. This steeping is sublime beyond measure, holding not just all the memories of all the *images* making up the World Soul but the full understanding of their symbolic meanings, as well. Interpenetrating with the primordial *images of psyche* at the Fount of the Center, one bears witness to the single generation of co-creators converting the *psychic substance* of the realm of pre-manifestation into the material form of the realm of manifestation. As a whole, this formula signifies that by stabilizing your intent to hold still in contentment, you are translated into an awe-struck witness within the unchanging eye of the storm of change.

INTENT

Bottom Line. Welcoming vitality: It circulates wildly between nature, human nature and the divine.

Second Line. Welcoming eternity: The unchanging smile of the infant.

Third Line. Welcoming work: Spiritual training raises the horizon.

Fourth Line. Welcoming pleasure: Ecstatic union is the root of creation.

Fifth Line. Welcoming reversal: The inner world revolves act upon act.

Top Line. Welcoming transmigration: Every thought is a new birth.

15

SHEDDING

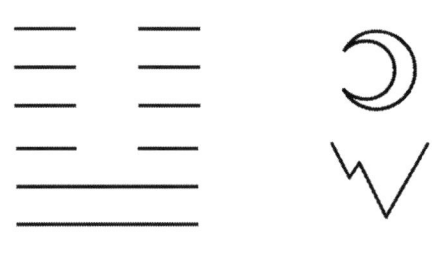

OUTER NATURE:	MOON
INNER NATURE:	LAKE

Lake within, Moon without: Wonder within, Completion without

Moon outside symbolizes completion of a cycle, while Lake inside symbolizes wonder. When an ordinary person completes their work, the time for celebration arrives. *Ordinary* in this sense means anyone, since all are equal in the eye of the *One*. *Completing a cycle,* likewise, means seeing a phase of development through successfully. Further, *Celebration* implies the spontaneous excitement and enduring enjoyment of one's path. From this perspective, the path of self-realization is open to all who approach the practice with buoyant light-heartedness. Those who are too serious or severe may lack the proper attitude to relinquish the ego-identity when the time comes.

The serpent is the living symbol of wisdom because it periodically sheds its skin in order to keep growing. The butterfly sheds its chrysalis as a living symbol of metamorphosis. Trees shed their leaves as a living symbol of seasonal renewal. *Shedding* is the natural and spontaneous sloughing-off of the old self during the process of spiritual rebirth.

This hexagram is paired with its complement, 48, EMBODYING.

HEXAGRAM SEQUENCE

After things have dreamed together, they wake together:
SHEDDING is embodying the bodiless.

The image of the *psychic substance* is that of the full moon reflected in a lake. This ancient symbol gives rise to the dictum, *One moon, many reflections*, which illustrates the fact that all the ponds in the world reflect the same moon at the same time. This ancient metaphor speaks directly to the truth-seeking soul: the full moon symbolizes the enlightened *One Mind*; all the ponds in the world symbolize all the individual bodies in the world of manifestation; the moon's reflection in every pond symbolizes the potential for immediate awakening among everybody in the world. Such awakening carries with it a profound shift of perspective, as the very sense of self with which one identifies one's whole life is suddenly shed, *with all the relief of peeling off a sweaty shirt,* and a radically different sense of self emerges. The subsequent process of identifying with this new sense of self is one aspect of what is meant by *embodying the bodiless*.

MANTIC FORMULA

Mountains and rivers, forest and sea:
You forget what you have become.

As years turn into decades, the new sense of self takes root, spreads its branches into the sky and puts forth fruit that carry its seeds into following generations. It becomes part of the landscape itself: within the pre-manifestation realm of the World Soul, yes, but also within the world of manifestation as others come to sit beside the bonfire one has kindled. One cannot genuinely identify with a sense of self that is essentially selfless—with the passage of time, the novelty of the selfless self wears thin and there is just this new, gleaming spirit serpent gliding across the land, grateful to be set free of the outworn skin. As a whole, this formula signifies that you merge with the whole of nature in the world of manifestation, fulfilling your intent within the World Soul to surrender the conditioned self to the ever-renewing, ever-shedding self of the anonymous soul.

INTENT

Bottom Line. Dreaming together: Cyclic rebirth is the soul's reward.

Second Line. Dreaming alone: Civilization is a caterpillar and the individual its chrysalis.

Third Line. Dreaming here: Cyclic rebirth is the body's initiation.

Fourth Line. Dreaming there: The past is a caterpillar and the present its chrysalis.

Fifth Line. Dreaming before: Cyclic rebirth is the ego's death.

Top Line. Dreaming after: Divinity is a caterpillar and the soul its chrysalis.

16

CONCEPTION

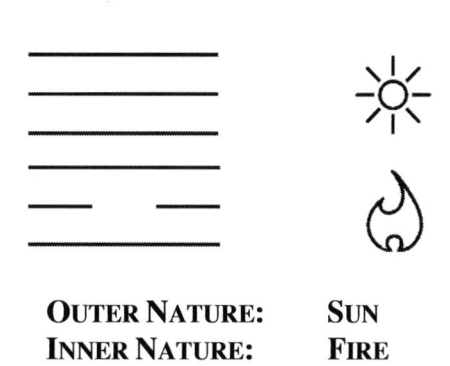

OUTER NATURE:	SUN
INNER NATURE:	FIRE

Fire within, Sun without: Knowledge within, Creation without

Sun outside symbolizes beginning, conception, while Fire inside symbolizes knowledge of the *law of spiritual cause and effect*. A previous cycle closes, a new one opens: ever the spiral turns toward greater realization. It begins with dreaming: human nature first encounters *psyche* in the strange and inexplicable mystery of dreams, wherein the *psychic substance* of their own Ancestral Memory exteriorizes itself into a spatial dimension of collapsed time. The dimensions of the dream-space reflect the individual's horizon of selfhood—the individual's awareness of extension of the soul, in other words. For the uninitiated, the beginning goes no further. But for the initiated, dreams provide an *angle of entry* into the oceanic *psychic substance* of the World Soul. The image-symbols of dreams, with their own intentions and significances, pave the way for the soul to encounter the living entities occupying and emerging from the background of *psychic substance* in the form of image-symbols with their own intentions and significances. It is in this atmosphere that the initiated begin to *conceive image-symbols* to which they will apply their intent with the goal of seeing them realized in the world of manifestation.

This hexagram is paired with its complement, 47, ENTRAINING.

Hexagram Sequence

After things have renewed themselves, they conceive themselves in a new light:
Conception is a spark of divine fire.

What stands between human nature and unimpeded, immediate entry into the World Soul is the conditioned self, fashioned by familial and cultural influences since birth. Most people find it hard to imagine that this sense of self, so conditioned by the historical era into which they are born, is not their real self—that there might be another, authentic and sovereign, self beneath the surface of the ego-identity appears ludicrous at first glance. Even more so when confronted with the idea that that deeper self is free of being unduly influenced by external circumstances. Yet, of course, it is the very conditioned self that finds such ideas nonsensical, for it has been trained to hold conventional thinking dear and all else fanciful imagination. For the initiated, though, the conditioned self is that which is to be surrendered at the *Great Death*, that point in the practice where the ego-identity is transcended in an act of self-remembering that spontaneously and immediately *transforms the act of identification*—without any internal resistance, the seat of pure awareness consciously re-identifies itself as the *original self*. With the covering of the conditioned self removed, awareness simply remembers its *original face before its parents ever met*. This original self is traditionally conceived as a spark of the divine fire of the *One* that incarnates in order to animate the body and to fulfill its trans-lifetime purpose.

Mantic Formula

Above and below reunite on the Summer Solstice:
Your fire is a little sun.

The original self and the conditioned self reflect one another perfectly at the height of intensity of awareness: the *Great Death* opens the way for the *Great Rebirth* of the original self. Recognizing itself as a unique *Idea* of the *One Mind*, the original self finds itself reflected in the diamond-like clarity of each and every other unique *Idea* of the *One Mind*—just as it is reflecting each and every other unique *Idea* of the *One Mind* at the same time. This simultaneous mutual reflection of all the unique *Ideas* allows for the full *memory* and *understanding* of each to pass into all. In this manner, no *Idea* is isolated from all the others, in the continuing creation of a matrix within which its diamond-like entities can continue to evolve in perfection. The unity of Ideas generates a web of relationships called the *law of spiritual cause and effect*, which establishes the transcendental order of evolving perfection as the emanations of the *One* pass through the realms of *pure idea*, *psychic substance* and *manifestation*. This transcendental order governs, among other relationships, the mechanism by which conception forms intent in the world of pre-manifestation and intent forms materialization in the world of manifestation. From *Above* to *Below*, the archetypal Idea traces its own footprints through the realms of increasingly denser *prima materia*. As a whole, this formula signifies that you internalize the *law of spiritual cause and effect*, your microcosmic fire of knowledge perfectly mirroring the macrocosmic sun of Truth.

INTENT

Bottom Line. Diamond fire: The great god Pan is alive and afoot.

Second Line. Diamond sun: The ancient gods and goddesses return to the Act of Creation.

Third Line. Diamond lightning: Humankind returns to the Garden of Eden.

Fourth Line. Diamond breath: The first Word reverberates still across the eons.

Fifth Line. Diamond light: The archangels stand like beacons on the edge of the Void.

Top Line. Diamond sea: The great goddess Venus embraces every soul in universal love.

17

BELONGING

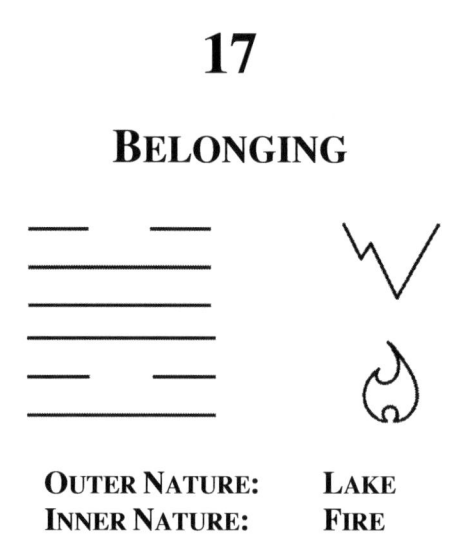

OUTER NATURE: LAKE
INNER NATURE: FIRE

Fire within, Lake without: Knowledge within, Wonder without

Lake outside symbolizes joyous communion, while Fire inside symbolizes knowledge based on direct first-hand experience. The *heart-mind* is a perfectly balanced paradox. It shifts back and forth between archetypal attentional spaces, a constant questing for all of the ways of *knowing* and of *being known*. For this is the essence of *belonging*: *knowing* and *being known*. Human nature certainly recognizes this in its person-to-person interactions, understanding that *somehow* people do come to know and be known by others—that without the mutual effort to reveal themselves to one another, they are isolated in their estrangement from their kind. To the initiated, as profoundly meaningful as such moments are, they are not the most profound experience of *belonging*, for human nature is but one facet of the threefold order of the world: *Nature, Human Nature* and *Spirit*. As meaningful as *belonging* is to human relationships, it takes on both a more personal *and* transpersonal aspect when applied to the sense of *belonging with* Nature and Spirit.

This hexagram is paired with its complement, 46, PRACTICE.

Hexagram Sequence

After things have advanced another stage, they find new allies:
Belonging is a gathering of angels.

Freedom of spirit and independence of movement are quintessential characteristics of a *real person*, but they are also the very traits that facilitate and govern the manner in which beings *belong together* and so form the alliances that contribute to the co-creation of the world. For this reason, autonomy is said to be the precursor to attracting allies—and alliances are said to be made up of nonmaterial bonds. Advance on the path brings the initiated into contact with higher order, nonmaterial beings, whose appearance is archetypal and whose presence is awe-inspiring. The development from conceiving an image-symbol to encountering its living form carries with it all the overtones of divine action, imbuing the intentions with the most profound desire to imitate the ancient gods and goddesses—the veil between what is imagined and what is revealed is forever rent, for what reveals itself to itself suffers no illusion. The initiated find themselves in a convocation of angelic beings, in a celestial choir, in a sense, whose song is a word, chanted over and over, until the great change it harbingers takes form in the world of manifestation.

Mantic Formula

The seed of gold is already present in the fruit of lead:
You stand at the gate of nondifferentiation.

Belonging with Nature: the breeze caresses the mountain pine, the shadow of the moon kisses the ocean tide, dragon lightning serenades the rain, the dervish bonfire praises the midnight sun. To be in nature is not the same as belonging with nature. To think about nature is not the same as belonging with nature. To withdraw the sense of self-importance and self-centeredness accompanying so much of human nature, to gratefully and voluntarily be just another rock, just another tree, just another blade of grass—to interpenetrate with the breeze, the moon, the dew, the clouds, the sun: this freedom to reenter the unchanging world of living matter as an intrinsic element of the whole, *this* is belonging with nature.

Belonging with Spirit: figures emerge from the mist, metamorphose constantly, settle into a breathing image, speak in thoughts of light. A fish dies and decomposes in the waters of the ocean it has lived in all its life, its decomposed body mingling thoroughly with the decomposed bodies making up much of the waters of the ancient ocean. Where does the fish end and the ocean begin? How can the fish and the ocean be two things? How can the *psyche* of the soul and the *psychic substance* of the World Soul be two things? The figure emerging from the mist, metamorphosing constantly, settling into a breathing image, speaking in thoughts of light, is oneself. Freely transforming around the pearl of living potential, the mist re-gathers, shimmers like moonlight on a river, sets fire to its nest, eats its own tail, bursts forth in a thousand constellations, evaporates in a dappled meadow, gathers again: ten thousand lifetimes in the blink of an eye, an infant's smile outlasts the tides—mist barely recognizing shape-shifting mist, oneself.

As a whole, this formula signifies that you *belong with* everything everywhere you go, the Great Wall between *knowing* and *being known* crumbled back to dust.

INTENT

Bottom Line. Deep accord: A generation of children worshipping nature.

Second Line. Deep accord: All cultures are created equal.

Third Line. Deep accord: An ally among great-souled beings.

Fourth Line. Deep accord: Magic paves the way for reason to advance.

Fifth Line. Deep accord: Listening to the teachers on all sides.

Top Line. Deep accord: Ideas have souls that play hide-and-seek.

18

CERTAINTY

OUTER NATURE:	FIRE
INNER NATURE:	FIRE

Fire within, Fire without: Knowledge within, Knowledge without

Fire outside symbolizes universal knowledge, while Fire inside symbolizes personal understanding. Fire needs wood in order to burn, knowledge needs experience in order to believe. Without first-hand realization, authentic certainty is impossible to achieve. However, it can be difficult to tell the difference between authentic certainty and that which is based opinion or conditioning—those who believe can look very much the same to an observer. For this reason, emphasis is not placed on discerning the validity of others' beliefs—rather, it is placed on questioning the validity of one's own beliefs. So long as people suffer from false certainty, they remain trapped in drinking from the mirage they have mistaken for an oasis. True certainty is the hallmark of the initiated, whose standpoint is based on personal realization of the reality underlying the world of appearances. It is not based on faith in any particular interpretation but, rather, on faith in one's own capacity to perceive, interpret and act on circumstances in appropriate, meaningful and constructive ways. For the initiated, this means internalizing the wisdom teachings of the ancients and testing them against the hardships of the historical era, discerning for themselves the enduring validity of the ancients' worldview.

This hexagram is paired with its complement, 45, UNCERTAINTY.

Hexagram Sequence

After things have formed new constellations, they settle into fixed orbits:
Certainty is faith in the genius of the true self.

The profound *intimacy* experienced by the initiated of *belonging with* the visible and invisible elements of Creation evokes both a deep-seated shift of awareness and a wide-ranging re-shaping of relationships. This deeper sense of *being with* the world and all its other elements reorients the *heart-mind* to the ecstatic act of communion with the Whole and its visible and invisible parts. This re-orientation is *not* a disorientation, however—while it changes one's perspective and awareness of emotional reality, it does so by establishing a *true* orientation. It is, as the ancients were fond of saying, *As if the compass points turned to correct themselves all at once*. This is true certainty, the aligning of one's heart with the One Heart, the first-hand experience of loving All Creation and of being loved by All Creation. It is as if the last tumbler in a combination lock fell into place: the true self finds its place in the emotional landscape of Creation. Here, it is not knowing things themselves, but the *relationships between things*, that establishes the *knowing* of the true self: understanding the archetypal relationships between things frees up the attendant spirit of deep intuition—direct knowing without recourse to discursive thinking—to recognize and interpret circumstances spontaneously, accurately and actionably. Faith in one's own genius avoids constant self-doubt and second-guessing one's conclusions: it provides the shortcut to responding immediately and congruently to circumstances by administering the appropriate measure and intensity of either *True Yin* or *True Yang*.

Mantic Formula

The mind feels when the heart knows:
You leave the path of thinking and return to the path of being.

Thinking is a valuable servant but a tyrant of a master. Whereas one may have *Being* without *Thinking*, one may not have *Thinking* without *Being*. What passes for education in modern societies is thinly-disguised cultural conditioning aimed at producing compliant workers already mentally trained to accept as given the worldview of their contemporaries—the means of transmitting such training is via *Thinking* and the goal of that training is to approach life via *Thinking*. Just as engaging in *Thinking* overshadows the state of *Being*, dwelling in the state of *Being* overshadows the activity of *Thinking*: *Being* is pure awareness devoid of producing thoughts, whereas *Thinking* produces the very thoughts that carry it away from *Being*. It is for this reason that the ancients summarized their relationship: *When Being moves, it becomes Thinking—when Thinking stops, it becomes Being.* Ultimately, *Thinking* rests on doubt, as it must constantly probe every possible argument in order to prove itself correct; a lifetime of doubt and criticism leaves a person with only one last thing to doubt—*doubt itself*—but by then, the habit of *Thinking* is so ingrained as to be practically irremediable.

The mind is not dedicated to Thinking by its very nature: it seeks the relationships between things and, once these are personally experienced, finds the emotional connection binding them. As a whole, this formula signifies that you discover for yourself the ancient correlation between *knowing* and *being known* and *loving* and *being loved*.

INTENT

Bottom Line. Soul making: The iron memory is the blacksmith's forge.

Second Line. Soul calling: Echoes from the eldest stars name the future.

Third Line. Soul making: Allies join mid-journey.

Fourth Line. Soul calling: Perfections incubating within heart-mind.

Fifth Line. Soul making: Two halves of a broken symbol reunited.

Top Line. Soul calling: Dreams teach all day long.

19

RELEARNING

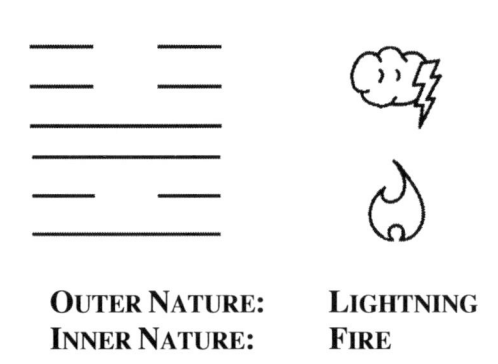

OUTER NATURE:	LIGHTNING
INNER NATURE:	FIRE

Fire within, Lightning without: Knowledge within, Motivation without

Lightning outside symbolizes an external incitement to change, while Fire inside symbolizes the clarity of self-awareness. Certainty about the essence of things gives rise to new learning about the existence of things—intimacy with the relationships between things gives rise to curiosity about things themselves. The movement now is in the direction of the world of manifestation, where manifold conditions offer untold opportunities to experience the world of appearances in profoundly meaningful ways. This path into the physical phenomena of the world permits the initiated to understand its mineral, vegetable and animal elements in new and exciting ways—more than that, though, it is a path that expands the initiate's skills and capacities in life. Relearning the ways of the world as a Living Being rather than a clockwork mechanism brings one's spiritual evolution into manifestation in the World Body.

This hexagram is paired with its complement, 44, IMPROVISATION.

Hexagram Sequence

After things have transcended doubt, they transcend truth:
RELEARNING is viewing the same light through a different facet.

The quest for truth leads beyond truth to reality. Mastering *Thinking* leads beyond itself, back into *Being*—with the passage of enough time in the timeless, *Being* moves, seeking activity and new views in the act of *Thinking*. It is the love of nature, in particular, that drives initiates back into the world of manifestation in order to relearn the real intricacies of the Living Body of the world—an investigation that shreds the materialistic worldview they were taught, replacing it with a clear-sighted vision of *The Miraculous* within which they dwell.

Mantic Formula

Mountains and rivers preach constantly:
You listen with the ears of tree and wolf.

To one who knows how to listen, the whole world is speaking moment-by-moment, extemporaneously reciting the epic poem of life and death, even as it is being lived. It is the howl of mortality, the sigh of autumn leaves, yes, but to one who knows how to listen, it is the chorus of collective ecstasy rising up through the night of sorrow, the crescendo of bittersweet memories swelling with the glory of gratitude and reverence for the miracle of life—and death. It is the materialistic worldview itself, so dedicated to the desecration of nature and human nature, that requires relearning: to listen with the ears of tree and wolf means that the World Body speaks in a language only its living cells understand. As a whole, this formula signifies that you discover for yourself that Form Itself is indeed the Beloved.

INTENT

Bottom Line. Fathoming volcano: The Angel of Earth displays itself.

Second Line. Fathoming summer: The Angel of Winter fans the flame.

Third Line. Fathoming thunder: The Angel of the Storm is the Word of Light.

Fourth Line. Fathoming night: The Angel of the Moon hides its face.

Fifth Line. Fathoming abyss: The Angel of the Sea calls the mermaids home.

Top Line. Fathoming fire: The Angel of Stars circles time backward.

20

TRADITION

OUTER NATURE:	WIND
INNER NATURE:	FIRE

Fire within, Wind without: Knowledge within, Adaptation without

Wind outside symbolizes adaptation to the historical era, while Fire inside symbolizes innate memory. Learning about the ways of nature on a deeper, more meaningful, level brings the initiated into a new stage of participation with nature—a stage that unites nature and human nature so as to participate in the spirit world in a deeper, more meaningful, way. As the footprint, so to speak, of spirit, nature provides the visible springboard by which human nature can bound into the invisible sea of spirit: by the footprint it is possible to draw analogies about the characteristics and behavior of that which made the footprint. Such was the approach of the ancients and most of the wisdom teachings they left behind derive directly from such analogies. The reviving of traditional worldviews promises to renew modern civilization by instilling within its increasingly meaningless activity a core of meaningful attitudes and behaviors that celebrate and ennoble all life. The ancient traditions are alive today because they reside in the universal memory of human nature, available to all who open their heart-mind to reawakening the ancient lifeway of harmonious balance between nature, human nature and spirit.

This hexagram is paired with its complement, 43, REFINING.

Hexagram Sequence

After things have established a wider context, they see the old ways anew:
Tradition is invisible ritual enacted in the visible.

To participate authentically in the world is to act and react ritually. Rituals are forms of concentration and reverence that gain potency through repeated enactment over time. Ritual is *not* empty form, the meaning of which has been lost, forgotten or ignored—it is an act of concentration and reverence that embodies the ancients' worldview. Such traditional rituals may not exhibit any recognizable external sign of being performed, but those attuned to the spirit of nature perceive their execution a thousand miles away. *Everything has a visible half and an invisible half. All of Nature is invested with Spirit. Every form is made up of many pairs of halves. Benefit All at the same time. Everything is sacred, so one must act like a sacred being among sacred beings. Everything is One and It has Intelligence. Death is the Winter of Transformation prior to the Rebirth of Spring's Renewal.* And so on. Such are the traditional wisdom teachings born of intimacy with nature and midwifed by spirit. It is *thought*, after all, that is ritualized.

Mantic Formula

The spirit of nature wakes from its dream:
You are a landmark against the sky.

The modern mind must turn itself inside-out to return to the original state of participation in the world that the ancients employed. This is because the modern mind has become the ego-centered subject of a subject-object worldview so pervasive that it precludes conscious entry into the *Living Unity* of Creation. The spirit of nature circulates within each thing and among all things. This it does in its dreaming state, translating the images of psyche into the living forms of manifestation. Occasionally, however, the spirit of nature awakens within one of its manifest forms, surrounded as it is by the rest of its dreaming self.

Awareness streams from form, like a signal fire atop a great column of stone, like an eternal flame deep within a mountain cavern, like lightning holding the night in thrall: the spirit of nature awakens to itself in the midst of its great dreaming—awareness gathers, coalesces, shape-shifts across the spectrum of image-symbols, finally to settle into self-identity. Into soul. Into oneself.

As a whole, this formula signifies that you revivify the world by bringing the deep mysteries of the old ones up the surface of the modern mind.

INTENT

Bottom Line. Yoke bearer: Before humankind and after humankind, eternal nature spirit.

Second Line. Yoke bearer: Ghosts of the ancient ones cannot be mistaken for ghosts.

Third Line. Yoke bearer: The higher soul acquits the lower soul.

Fourth Line. Yoke bearer: Mystical conjunction of sea and sky celebrated in nightly reflection.

Fifth Line. Yoke bearer: The moon-pearl cultivated inside the sky-sea.

Top Line. Yoke bearer: A divine child born of water-sea and fire-sky.

21

RATIONALITY

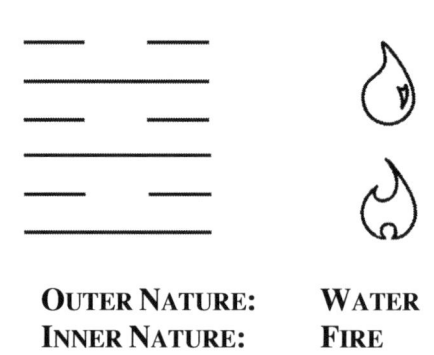

OUTER NATURE: WATER
INNER NATURE: FIRE

Fire within, Water without: Knowledge within, Mystery without

Water outside symbolizes the Great Mystery of Creation, while Fire inside symbolizes conscious knowledge. Embodying the ancients' wisdom teachings in thought, word and action makes apparent the bridge between the mystic and the rational. Ritualizing thought in accord with the inherent mysticism of the soul opens the bridge to a deeper understanding of the soul's logic in the art of manifestation. This art develops from the encounter between the Great Mystery and the individual intelligence: though the Great Mystery is part of *The Already*, aspects of Creation already present prior to the self-awareness of the individual intelligence, the personal intellect must grow and evolve through direct experience of the world beyond it. This is particularly true of its coming-to-know the Great Mystery, the *Living Sphinx*, whose very nature is an unanswerable question and yet who's very being is impossible to avoid. Therefore, the surest road to *rational mysticism* is taking up the path of the ancients' teachings, following them into the realm of *psychic substance* and incorporating thereby the *law of spiritual cause-and-effect* into the individual intelligence.

This hexagram is paired with its complement, 42, IRRATIONALITY.

Hexagram Sequence

After things have upheld the mystic lineage, they reveal a deeper logic:
Rationality is the secret eye of spiritual cause-and-effect.

The lifeway of the ancients is an inner path that leads to the inner world. That it is enacted in the outer world is not always a given, as that depends in part on the historical era into which one is born. The inner world, the Spirit World, has laws that govern it no less than the laws of physics govern the material world. The *law of spiritual cause-and-effect* applies first and foremost to the relationship between the World Soul and the World Body: archetypal causes in the pre-manifestation realm give rise to specific effects in the manifestation realm. Such causes, furthermore, are intentional in nature, the crystalized attention of the soul, which gives rise to images that shape the *psychic substance* of the World Soul into manifest effects within the World Body—archetypal intentions such as *metamorphosis and inertia*, for example, manifest as specific *change and continuity* in the world of effects. Moreover, the greater the intensity of intent, the greater the likelihood of it taking effect in the manifestation realm—in general, this means that the greater number of souls concentrating on an archetypal image-symbol, the greater the chance of it taking effect; there are exceptions to this, however, as there are souls whose individual intent is so potent—or produces an image-symbol of such surprising thrust—that they are able to trigger their desired effect without collaboration.

Mantic Formula

The soul throws one backward:
You transmute the lead of reason into the gold of wisdom.

The World Soul does not have a conscience. It is the realm of pure *psyche*, whose substance may take the form of the full range of diversity-in-manifestation. It is neither good or evil in itself but, like clay, takes whatever form intended by the artist. This, of course, is the reason the world of manifestation swings between Ages of Light and Dark: the intentions of souls manifest their nature in the historical eras of the World Body. The current transition from an Age of Darkness to an Age of Light makes clear how volatile manifestations become as intentions reach extremes of both values and intensity. As souls transform in their values, the vast majority will seek very different manifestations than the current consensus—fear, for so long, has coursed through the majority of souls in the World Soul, that it has caused a backlash of self-interest, greed, hostility and self-destruction in the World Body. The Darkness is not a metaphor: it is a presence that lays upon the World Soul, like a fog of threat to the soul itself, that sets in motion a cycle of deep-seated fear among the greater number of souls, propelling them into reactionary values that manifest great suffering in the World Body. The Light, similarly, is not a metaphor: it is a presence that lays upon the World Soul, like a change of climate to warmth, sunlight, and plenitude that propels the greater number of souls into manifesting a growing time of peace and prospering for all. It is true nonetheless that even at the height of an Age of Darkness, there are souls intending manifestations of the brightest light possible—just as at the height of an Age of Light, there are souls intending manifestations of the darkest shadow possible. The upshot of the law of spiritual cause-and-effect, then, is that noble-minded and great-hearted souls need *always* form alliances in the pre-manifestation realm in order to collaborate on a common intent to bring the most benefit to all within the world of manifestation.

As a whole, this formula signifies that you revert to the inner path, following it all the way back into the inner landscape of *rational mysticism*, which transcends base reason through first-hand experience of the celestial wisdom embodying the universal *law of spiritual cause-and-effect*.

INTENT

Bottom Line. World tree: Angel logic governs the true spheres.

Second Line. World tree: A pebble in a distant pond casts ripples in a nearby pond.

Third Line. World tree: Ritual draws the immortal into the temporal.

Fourth Line. World tree: The vanguard angels beckon from the coming Age.

Fifth Line. World tree: Shadows do not lead, they follow.

Top Line. World tree: The road of stars carries the souls of the dead to the spirit world.

22

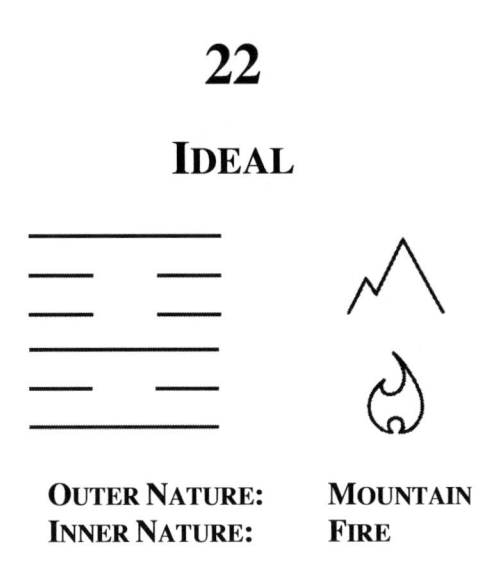

IDEAL

OUTER NATURE:	MOUNTAIN
INNER NATURE:	FIRE

Fire within, Mountain without: Knowledge within, Incubation without

Mountain outside symbolizes an external standstill, while Fire inside symbolizes self-awareness. It is as if the great forces of fire and molten rock were bottled up inside a mountain and not allowed to erupt. Mountains are the longest-lasting of earthly phenomena and the fiery magma welling up from the earth's core is the oldest, original, earthly material. This Mountain is the height of the earthly surface and this Fire is the depth of the earthly interior—together, they symbolize the most ancient of creative forces, their self-sustaining natures and their extremities. For the soul, this is the image-symbol of the longed-for ideal state of harmonious repose and spiritual contemplation: withdrawn from external influences as if in a monastery, abiding in quiet tranquility like a savant in deep meditation—ever exploring new heights and new depths, the initiated make the most of this time of extending the limits of awareness.

This hexagram is paired with its complement, 41, CONTENTMENT.

Hexagram Sequence

After things have aligned with divine order, they embody their ideal nature:
IDEAL is witnessing perfection within.

The divine order reveals itself in the *law of spiritual cause-and-effect*, making clear how matters in the world of manifestation are seeded and evolve—but, beyond that, it points at how the pre-manifestation realm is seeded and evolves by dint of emanations from the world of *Pure Idea* that stands between the *One* and the *World Soul*. This realm of *Pure Idea* is the *Ideal World*, the realm of original archetypes prior to their densification in the realm of *psyche*: prior to taking form as image-symbols in *psychic substance*, pure ideas embody the perfected, eternal and relatively unchanging nature of the One Mind. The most obvious example of pure ideas is that of *Number*, which, despite being applied to an infinite number of usages, is never changed of its eternal character. *Pure Idea*, however, does not imply soulless abstractions—the ancient savant, Pythagoras, for example, left this wisdom teaching for the ages: *Every number has a soul*. And so it is with every *Divine Idea* of the *One Mind*. Each is a being, more subtle and more powerful than its embodiment in *psyche*, but recognizable, approachable and responsive. These eternal beings, closer to the *One* than all others, are living archetypes of the highest order, the original *messengers* of Divine Mind, the primordial *harbingers* of transformation: the archangels they are called, for their presence is of the same order as that of the ancient gods and goddesses. The inner path through the *World Soul* into the realm of *Pure Idea* can only be navigated by those with the capacity to perceive their inner perfections.

Mantic Formula

A necklace of perfect moments:
You are time.

To step into the *Ideal World* is to shed every memory of imperfections, for this is the realm of *First Creations*, still existing at the primordial Act of Creation in its pristine and original wholeness. The initiated can sense this path, though it seems at the edge of a vast fogbank sprawled to the horizon—it is the higher soul, the *celestial soul*, that maintains the half-remembered bond between *Psyche* and *Nous*, between the *World Soul* and the world of *Pure Idea*. When the higher soul identifies with its work with the *psychic substance* of the World Soul, then it stands between the pre-manifestation realm and the manifestation realm; when the higher soul identifies with its original nature as a unique *Idea* of the *One Mind*, then it stands between the world of *Psyche* and the world of *Pure Idea*. To shed every memory of imperfection is an act of both personal and universal amnesia: beginning with what is nearby, the initiated behold their own inner perfections—only after this perception is stabilized are they able to extend it to beholding the perfection of each of the other unique *Ideas* of the *Ideal World*. Communing with other *Divine Ideas*, the initiated stands at the furthest edge of the *Ideal World*, all but fully-returned to the *Sphere of Universal Communion* of the *One*. As a whole, this formula signifies that you awaken to the *Divine Thought* flowing through all the unique *Ideas* at once in its stream of emanation passing into the timeless realm of *psyche* and thence into the fully-realized timebound realm of manifestation.

INTENT

Bottom Line. Hidden counsels: The fire of desecration completely extinguished and its ashes scattered.

Second Line. Hidden counsels: A garden without weeds.

Third Line. Hidden counsels: The purest gold from the hottest fire.

Fourth Line. Hidden counsels: The angelic nature knows no doubt.

Fifth Line. Hidden counsels: Master and student exchange places.

Top Line. Hidden counsels: The line of least resistance produces the charisma of fortune.

23

NONINTERFERENCE

OUTER NATURE: MOON
INNER NATURE: FIRE

Fire within, Moon without: Knowledge within, Completion without

Moon outside symbolizes completion, while Fire inside symbolizes knowledge. The high road of ethical behavior—in every world—is a steepness and narrowness beside abyss and through pass: it takes wisdom, experience and empathy to know how to avoid interfering in others' fate without abandoning them to something worse. For doing nothing may be as much of an interference as any intervening action. This Fire of necessary wisdom, experience and empathy is finally completed through this Moon of cyclic time, resulting eventually in the perfect poise and equilibrium from which to act with the highest ethic: *angelic noninterference*.

This hexagram is paired with its complement, 40, DEESCALATING.

HEXAGRAM SEQUENCE

After things have glimpsed the end, they develop of their own accord:
NONINTERFERENCE is the path of archangels.

Those who perceive the *Ideal World* know first-hand that all things are evolving from *perfect origin* to *perfect destination*, so long as their natural course suffers no interference. Obviously, that fortuitous state occurs much less often than otherwise, since the course from *alpha* to *omega* is long and the uninitiated many. *To suffer no interference*: from the time of the ancients to the yet-to-be generations, nothing has been simpler to promise nor more difficult to achieve. The ancients knew that a balanced and harmonious life required self-control, especially when it pertained to nature and human nature. To fit society into the niche nature holds for it—that is the lifeway of harmony. To accommodate others and be accommodated by others—that is the lifeway of balance. To interfere with nature and disrupt its perfect cycle of renewal, to interfere with others and disrupt their intrinsic wellbeing—that is the lifeway of self-destruction. From the perspective of the world of manifestation, therefore, the very concept of *angelic noninterference* seems impossible to achieve, for all modern efforts to remediate these long-held habits of self-destruction are futile and wither on the vine. But from the perspective of the World Soul, the causes of these self-destructive manifestations are clear and reparable: too many souls lost in darkness and fear, concentrating their intentions on the mirage of danger instead of the oasis of freedom. Still, it remains difficult to persuade the soul disoriented and confused within the shifting tides of *psychic substance* of its misperception and correct re-orientation—it is only by the first-hand experience of the *Ideal World* beyond the *World Soul* that the soul sees through the illusion of perceived threats and into the heart of universal freedom.

MANTIC FORMULA

The soul draws emptiness close:
You are able to pivot in any direction.

Freedom means free of undue influence: noninterference. This raises the question, of course, of whether one can achieve this state of mind despite concerted external interference. The traditional answer is that it is possible, that it constitutes a praxis handed down in the ancients' wisdom teachings—but, speaking from the other side of the veil, those ancients remind their descendants that such should not, realistically, be necessary, since universal noninterference requires much less effort. To achieve that, though, the soul must gain entry into the *Ideal World*, which it does by authentically perceiving the perfections of things, including itself. This it accomplishes via the backward method.

To follow the law of spiritual cause-and-effect *forward* is to bear witness to the spiritual cause of material manifestations. Following the law of spiritual cause-and-effect *backward*, however, uncovers the spiritual cause of *psyche* among the *Pure Ideas*—and reflects the work of returning manifestations to the *One*. Manifestations seem on the surface to be more real than symbols in the pre-manifestation realm—but the art of returning manifestations to the *One* involves reifying them further *into symbols* of eternally-evolving perfection reflecting their earlier origin in the realm of *Pure Idea*. Carrying the symbol back to the Act of Creation, the soul gains entry to the *Ideal World* and grasps, in an instant, the utter, fundamental, unassailable relationship between the mirage of illusion and the oasis of truth. As a whole, this formula signifies that you experience all the barriers falling away from the vast expanse of open potential— unrestricted by any undue influences, you achieve absolute freedom of thought, feeling and action.

INTENT

Bottom Line. Blissful standstill: No progress, no striving, no destruction.

Second Line. Blissful training: The practice embodies the ecstatic life.

Third Line. Blissful virtue: The lower soul creates benefit.

Fourth Line. Blissful peace: A harmonious civilization creates no history.

Fifth Line. Blissful custom: A people exercising self-control.

Top Line. Blissful genius: The higher soul creates beauty.

24

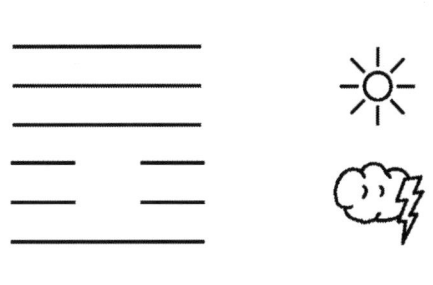

FOUNDING

OUTER NATURE:	SUN
INNER NATURE:	LIGHTNING

Lightning within, Sun without: Motivation within, Creation without

Sun outside symbolizes a new beginning, while Lightning inside symbolizes driving intent. Who would image the giant redwood tree secreted within the tiny seed? Yet, the seed does not appear out of thin air—it falls from the previous generation of giants, a concentrated intention to continue the lineage. So it is with *founding*: the humblest of beginnings, secreted within the sincerest of rituals, beneath the notice of all but the ancient gods and goddesses—nothing but a sacred intent seeking to continue a lineage of giants, an unstoppable force if fallen on fertile ground.

This hexagram is paired with its complement, 39, INDIVIDUALITY.

Hexagram Sequence

After things have accepted universal peace, they conceive a cradle:
Founding is planting the seed of paradise.

With a vision of a balanced and harmonious lifeway in heart-mind, the initiated collaborate in fashioning an intent of such beauty, grace and dignity that ever more souls gather to contribute their *righteous intent* to its full realization in the world of manifestation. This *founding ritual* in the World Soul is a continuous act of concentrating spiritual desire into a material *Golden Age*, conceived as an enduring time of universal peace and prospering for all peoples, in which humanity lives in true and meaningful harmony with nature. Such a *founding* contains all the elements of inevitability that the tiny seed does when fallen upon fertile ground: it unleashes an unstoppable force into the world of manifestation, one that bridges the long-distant previous *Age of Light* with the coming one.

Mantic Formula

Traversing the abyss of shadow:
You radiate only benefit for all.

The course between *alpha* and *omega* is long and the uninitiated are many: the World Soul is still held in sway by the last vestiges of the *Age of Shadow*, the larger part of souls still disoriented and pursuing the mirage instead of the oasis. The initiated are like horses with blinders on—they look neither to the right nor to the left, but straight ahead without becoming distracted by the *shadow intents* of those groups of souls conjuring war, violence, poverty, hatred, greed, self-destruction and desecration of the environment within the world of manifestation. As the ancients were fond of saying, *Passing through a village with a poisoned well, the wise do not take a single sip.* The lightning bolt of *righteous intent* within grants no entry to *shadow thoughts* from without. As a whole, this formula signifies that you contribute to the coming *Golden Age* by maintaining strict concentration on the single intent, *To Benefit All*.

INTENT

Bottom Line. Umbilical renewal: Souls come on the Spring Equinox and go on the Autumnal Equinox.

Second Line. Umbilical sustenance: Allies concoct the antidote to anxiety and discord.

Third Line. Umbilical principle: The star in human nature guides the subtle body home.

Fourth Line. Umbilical return: A community based upon the ancients' wisdom teachings.

Fifth Line. Umbilical power: A society existing for the individual to realize potential.

Top Line. Umbilical marriage: Souls uniting lifetime after lifetime.

25

ALLIANCE

OUTER NATURE:	LAKE
INNER NATURE:	LIGHTNING

Lightning within, Lake without: Motivation within, Wonder without

Lake outside symbolizes communion, while Lightning inside symbolizes inspiration. The World Soul has various names—*the Dreamtime, the Spirit World, the In-Between World, the Imaginal, the Nagual.* Souls of similar intent within that pre-manifestation world join together to add greater power and coherence to an image-symbol they are sending into the world of manifestation. Such an *alliance* of souls is based upon a shared common inspiration and a sense of close trust and bonding, which results in a web of relationships stretching over long periods of time and many lifetimes in the manifestation world. Alliances such as these are not limited to their interactions in the World Soul, however, as they often involve continued mutual support as some or all of its allies enter the world of manifestation in order to further the work of materialization.

This hexagram is paired with its complement, 38, PROTECTING.

Hexagram Sequence

After things have dedicated the endeavor, they form a pact:
ALLIANCE is visible help from the invisible.

Souls who entered the manifestation realm must remain vigilant for signs of assistance from their alliance within the World Soul. Depending on the upbringing and social conditioning to which they have been exposed, it may require diligent practice to develop the sensitivity to recognize and make use of such assistance. This *visible help from the invisible* is not something that can be sought or evoked—it is coming through a membrane of shifting complexity that reduces *timeless intent* to its denser form of *timebound reification*: just as it may take light from a star hundreds of years to reach Earth, such invisible help fully entering the visible has its own sense of timing. A second, more specific form of allies occurs as a result of *soul pacts* undertaken within the World Soul: members of an alliance agree to meet and assist one another at crucial moments within the world of manifestation. These *soul pacts* are matters of profound significance and grave consequence—to not reciprocate others' assistance, or even offer assistance to a stranger without understanding why, is not only self-defeating in the manifestation realm but disrupts the sacred nature of the alliance within the World Soul.

Mantic Formula

All the spokes of the wheel join at the axle:
You turn as one.

All the souls making up the alliance are concentrated around the central image-symbol they are attempting to introduce into the manifestation realm. This act of concentration does not begin with the effort to translate the symbol into manifestation—rather, it begins with the effort to *read* the symbol as conceived, understanding that it is preceded in Creation by its archetype. To grasp a symbol in its relationship to the whole of Creation is to read its original meaning as it derives from the realm of *Pure Idea* and, therefore, is invested with the archangels' nature as divine messengers, harbingers, of what is to come. The uninitiated cannot help but mistrust the concept of angels and archangels because of their preconceptions about them; but let them use their active imagination to visualize an archangel floating in the air before them and they begin to see the power of the archetype and its presence in *psychic substance*. To not rely completely on one's own power, but to draw upon the secret power of the symbol—this is the art of translating the symbol into manifestation. As a whole, this formula signifies that you are part of a great alliance of noble allies whose trans-lifetime work in the manifestation realm perfectly mirrors its unity of desire and single-minded purpose within the world of pre-manifestation.

INTENT

Bottom Line. Kindred spirits: Trees, rivers, mountains and clouds sanctify humankind.

Second Line. Kindred dreams: Souls take refuge in spiritual light during times of material darkness.

Third Line. Kindred grievances: Correcting wrong-doing without doing wrong.

Fourth Line. Kindred purpose: One with divine intent is a majority.

Fifth Line. Kindred mettle: Great-souled beings do not trivialize their lifetimes.

Top Line. Kindred cradle: Establishing the endeavor in the timeless.

26

ENNOBLING

OUTER NATURE:	FIRE
INNER NATURE:	LIGHTNING

Lightning within, Fire without: Motivation within, Knowledge without

Fire outside symbolizes acquired knowledge, while Lightning inside symbolizes inner breakthrough. From within the world of manifestation, it can be said that, *At first, Form adores Form; later, as it evolves, Form adores the Formless; in the end, the Formless adores Form.* The visible and invisible thus perform the eternal dance of *The Beloved*, so that from completely different perspectives and experiences, *The Beloved* returns to *Form* in the end. The visible, manifest, world can easily be perceived as lesser than, or secondary to, the invisible spirit world—this certainly happens as the uninitiated mature and become more familiar with the concepts of spirituality. The initiated, however, standing in the invisible World Soul, witness the grandeur and glory of the manifestation world as the miraculous incarnation of the spirit world—every dew-dropped leaf, every stippled egg, every infant's smile: nothing can prepare the awakened soul for its first glimpses of divine intent made flesh. *Form Itself is The Beloved*—a standpoint from which the rest of All Creation is raised that much higher.

This hexagram is paired with its complement, 37, POTENTIALITY.

Hexagram Sequence

After things have joined forces, they raise each above the other:
Ennobling is honoring purity of intent.

Souls who engage in a *soul pact* within the World Soul, vowing to meet when incarnated within the realm of manifestation in order to assist one another on their spiritual journeys, find that their interaction is not always restricted to brief episodes of helping one another—sometimes their pacts result in intense emotional relationships that last years, if not lifetimes. Such spiritual allies honor one another above all other human beings, treating them as angelic beings with the pure intent of living *Ideas*. Each places the other above them, serving them as the embodiment of the *One*. Such ennobling of the other is an act of ennobling one's own soul *and* body, for to act so in the world of manifestation is to build a monument towering above the horizon of self-interest, self-centeredness and self-importance. *Soul pacts* of such a nature are based on a sense of trust that arises from a shared purity of intent *to ever renew the spirit medicine flowing into the world from the pre-manifestation realm.*

Mantic Formula

The soul throws one upward:
You steal fire from the gods for the good of humankind.

Some *soul pacts* lead one to a teacher, someone so in accord with one's own soul that it seems as though both share the same soul. This an extraordinary relationship, one in which one's trust and respect are tested, just as metal is heated, pounded into shape, cooled, heated, and so on, by the blacksmith—the ancient art of tempering, whereby metal is made both stronger *and* more flexible. To place oneself in the hands of a true teacher is to feel as if one's soul has cast one into the sky, into the presence of great-souled beings whose common purpose is to demonstrate their *Love of The Beloved* in all its diversity and pandemonium. As a whole, this formula signifies that you take your place in a long lineage of those who walk among the ancient gods and goddesses in order to extract from them the secret recipe for the *spiritual medicine of immortality*.

INTENT

Bottom Line. Quickened moment: It is nature that awakens.

Second Line. Quickened moment: It is the shadow that awakens.

Third Line. Quickened moment: It is the memory that awakens.

Fourth Line. Quickened moment: It is lightning that awakens nature.

Fifth Line. Quickened moment: It is lightning that awakens the shadow.

Top Line. Quickened moment: It is lightning that awakens memory.

27

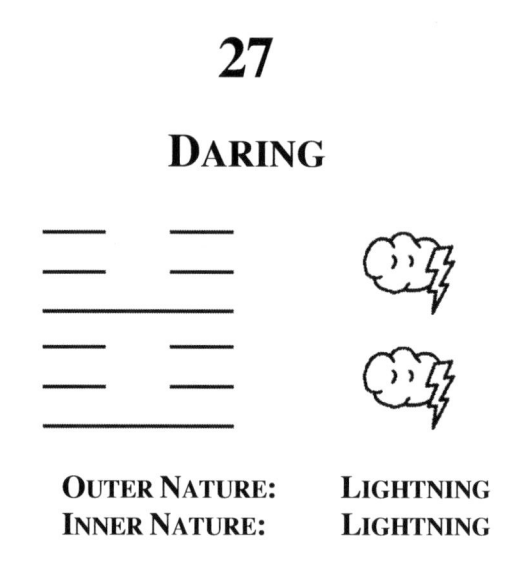

DARING

OUTER NATURE:	LIGHTNING
INNER NATURE:	LIGHTNING

Lightning within, Lightning without: Motivation within, Motivation without

Lightning outside symbolizes aspiration, while Lightning inside symbolizes aspiration. Great allies aspire to great achievements. When one's allies' aspirations are as lofty as one's own, the collaboration takes aim at provoking great change. Within the pre-manifestation realm of the World Soul, the alliance must remain sensitive to the stagnating intentions of the counter-Creation, whose penchant for self-destruction turns readily upon others when greed, hatred, hostility, self-interest and wanton desecration are threatened—direct attack creates backlash in the intentional realm, so it is wisest to dare to leapfrog over opponents by emanating intentions promising them greater *benefit* than they could themselves ever imagine. They are successful in their manipulation of *psychic substance* because it is the nature of the World Soul to fill great need and it is the soul-hunger of such beings that grants them—counter as it is to the whole of Creation—entryway into the world of manifestation. True daring addresses the root of discord by conceiving intentions that fulfill the soul-hunger of others even as they restore balance and harmony to the manifestation realm.

This hexagram is paired with its complement, 36, RESILIENCE.

HEXAGRAM SEQUENCE

After things have demonstrated affinity, they act with abandon:
DARING is the vanguard of change.

Within the World Body of the manifestation realm, great allies generate high hopes and fearless dreams. There is a sense of inevitability and rightness to the alliance's objectives that inspires it to throw caution to the wind and charge ahead with confidence and determination. Under many circumstances, this might prove fool-hardy and ill-advised, but the momentum of *intentional manifestation* supports just such a wild and exuberant victory march into the capital. It is just this sense of fatedness that attracts one's contemporaries to the undertaking, providing a groundswell of support for, and expectations of, freedom from long-standing desecration of nature and human nature. Omens and signs precede the arrival of such an alliance, just like the wind sweeps the streets ahead of the rain—the fortress collapses because it is besieged from within by the forces of self-destruction.

MANTIC FORMULA

Above and below form a single body:
You transform poison into medicine.

The alliance comprises the *psychic substance* above and the manifestation below, the concentrated intents of allied souls above and the inspired actions of the initiated below—spanning both worlds, the alliance works simultaneously to restore the sense of wholeness and open possibilities of *The Original*, of the earlier times in which human nature walks hand-in-hand with the ancient gods and goddesses—works above and below simultaneously to return to a lifeway, a way of *being present in the world*, embodied by the ancients in their direct perception of *Nature As Spirit* and *Human Nature As Spirit* and the true duty of every person is to *act as a sacred being among all other sacred beings*. It is the great daring of the alliance to reawaken this original presence within the modern world. As a whole, this formula signifies that you work simultaneously in both worlds to restore *Shadow* to its rightful and original harmonious balance with *Light*.

Intent

Bottom Line. Untroubled dreams: All this beauty is the ruins of an earlier world.

Second Line. Untroubled dreams: All this beauty will be the ruins of a later world.

Third Line. Untroubled dreams: Great-souled beings do not play with figures of mud in the dark.

Fourth Line. Untroubled dreams: History is the time between Golden Ages.

Fifth Line. Untroubled dreams: Innocents tearing down the gates of Heaven and Hell.

Top Line. Untroubled dreams: The entire play takes place among the gods and goddesses.

28

RESTORATION

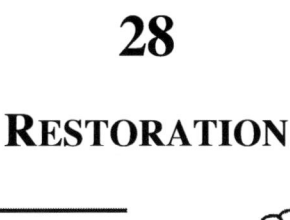

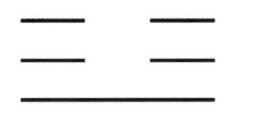

OUTER NATURE:	WIND
INNER NATURE:	LIGHTNING

Lightning within, Wind without: Motivation within, Adaptation without

Wind outside symbolizes adapting to circumstances, while Lightning inside symbolizes a shock. When stasis and stagnation are broken up and energy released back into circulation, the tendency among the uninitiated is to revert as quickly as possible to a state of comfortable equilibrium—people will sacrifice the greater portion of their joy of life in order to gain stability and security. Such is not true balance and harmony, which is in actuality a dynamic equilibrium continually moving between elements, often in the form of dualities. The initiated consider this closely when restoring things to a *Living Whole*.

This hexagram is paired with its complement, 35, PROPAGATION.

Hexagram Sequence

After things have shattered stagnation, they restore the valuable:
RESTORATION is the secret continuity of the meaningful.

Within the World Soul, Wind is the symbol of *Order*, while Lightning is the symbol of *Chance*. Wind moves in a direction and, though, invisible, makes its presence—and its passage—known by its effects. Lightning strikes without warning, utterly unpredictable, the timeless embodiment of chaos. Ultimately, every act of restoration is an act of reunifying *Order* and *Chance* in a new and dynamic way in order that they might find an equilibrium that bridges the ephemeral divide between the *Act of Creation* and the *Present Crossroads*: it is ever a unique mixture of intent spanning the abyss between *initial perfection* and *forward momentum*. Striving to maintain that original balance and harmony between *cultivated* and *wild*, the initiated understand that their own intents must reflect the ever-changing, ever-spontaneous, marriage of *the known* and *the unknown*.

What is easy to lose is the meaningful—what is easy to forget is that it is the meaningful that is valuable. *Meaning* is the sparks that fly from the clash of *the known* and *the unknown*—it is the child of the *ancient memory* of initial perfection and the *present decision* of forward momentum. It is the ever-changing, ever-spontaneous, ritual dance of the *Angel of Order* and the *Angel of Chance*.

Mantic Formula

A total eclipse of the sun:
You turn the handle of the pole star.

Even the most extreme balance between light and dark—a total eclipse of the sun—is harmonious and natural. Even the most extraordinary act imaginable—turning the sky by the handle of the pole star—is based on an inner equilibrium of symbols that maintain a straight-line continuity to the ancients through the wisdom teachings they bequeathed their descendants. The *Elixir Of Life* boils and condenses repeatedly in the alchemical retort of the soul's intent: measuring *Shadow* and *Light* in ever-changing, ever-spontaneous, lots, the soul scours the World Soul for the secret ingredients to increase the potency of the *spiritual medicine*. The secret of *Restoration* cannot be set in fixed rules or recipes—it can only be rediscovered in the *original intuition* of the soul who perceives *symbol* and *meaning* as one. As a whole, this formula signifies that you become spiritual medicine.

INTENT

Bottom Line. Reviving intimacy: A tidal wave of souls identify with nature's original spirit.

Second Line. Reviving symmetry: A tidal wave of souls meet in the middle, escaping all polarization.

Third Line. Reviving inheritance: A tidal wave of souls initiated by the ordeal of self-sacrifice.

Fourth Line. Reviving exultation: A tidal wave of souls reliving the primordial Act of Creation.

Fifth Line. Reviving conversion: A tidal wave of souls emerging from their chrysalis together.

Top Line. Reviving revolution: A tidal wave of souls reincarnate as enlightened children.

29

RESOLVE

OUTER NATURE: **WATER**
INNER NATURE: **LIGHTNING**

Lightning within, Water without: Motivation within, Mystery without

Water outside symbolizes the Great Mystery, while Lightning inside symbolizes inspiration. Those who revere the *Angel of Chance* as they do the *Angel of Order* cast open the vault of the Great Mystery, loosing upon All Creation the full force of the *Coming Unknown*. The uninitiated react with fear and dread at the approaching storm and all it will carry away. The initiated respond from the center of the storm, in awe and ecstasy at the *unforeseen new* unbalancing the old. The alliance grows astronomically to surge through the World Soul like a desert sand storm scouring everything clean again. No one but nomads move with the storm—no one but sedentaries lose their place. Souls move or stay by intent—if not their own, then a greater intent cobbled and fused together of all the intents bent on fulfilling the common need.

This hexagram is paired with its complement, 34, REFLECTING.

Hexagram Sequence

After things have passed through the ordeal, they strengthen their purpose:
RESOLVE is impossible to unnerve.

Souls are immortal and yet they fear. They seldom know specifically what they fear because what they fear is *The Unknown*. The nature of the *psychic substance* is malleable, more so than a dream because there are many more intents interacting, and so it is unpredictable—often to an extreme. The contents of a dream can turn nightmarish, more by the emotional overtones of a threat than any real threat; likewise, a person may be sitting comfortably in their home reading a book and be carried away by the story, becoming overwhelmingly frightened by emotions called up from within. So it is in the realm of *psyche*, where contagion from other souls leaks in, creating an emotional atmosphere of impending peril and menace. It is possible for such an atmosphere to endure in the World Soul for long cycles, coloring the mood with shadows of foreboding and danger. This state, of course, given its intensity, is all too easily translated into the manifestation realm.

Souls are immortal and have nothing to fear. *Resolve* takes its stand at the center of immortality, casting all extraneous thoughts aside. The indestructible has nothing to fear, it is impossible to unnerve.

Mantic Formula

The eye of the storm is the unchanging center around which revolves all change:
You hold the stillpoint of grace.

To carry *Resolve* into the world of manifestation is one of the greatest tests for a soul. Wrapped in the coil of mortality, human nature is ever more exposed to events reinforcing the death of the body and ever less to events reminding the soul of its deathlessness. Pain and suffering and the death of others wear like iron chains on the uninitiated, slowly eroding their souls' memories of their lives in the World Soul. *Resolve*, in the manifestation realm, is held in heart-mind like a sacred jewel that bestows the secret memories of life beyond the world—in this sense, it is not so much a matter of casting off all doubts and fears, but of remaining poised in identification with the unchanging center of the world storm of change: it is from within the silence of this center that the eternal voice of the sacred jewel can be heard. As a whole, this formula signifies that you advance through this lifetime with a sense of purpose and inevitability that remains untarnished by unease or distress to the very end.

INTENT

Bottom Line. Lunar fireball: Giants stalk the land, healing wounded dreams.

Second Line. Tidal fireball: The society that fails to serve the individual fails itself.

Third Line. Blinding fireball: The rational mind is the most useful tool in the mystic's toolkit.

Fourth Line. Embracing fireball: No obstacle is insurmountable to a dedicated band of immortals.

Fifth Line. Scrying fireball: Only the emptiness of mind is vast enough to contain the universe entire.

Top Line. Solar fireball: The way back to the Origin is the same road to the Destination.

30

METAMORPHOSIS

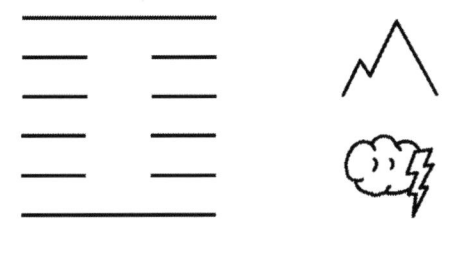

OUTER NATURE: MOUNTAIN
INNER NATURE: LIGHTNING

Lightning within, Mountain without: Motivation within, Incubation without

Mountain outside symbolizes tranquility and containment, while Lightning inside symbolizes energy and activity. The image is that of a chrysalis: on the outside, a containment vessel and, on the inside, an abundance of energetic activity—the living symbol of that which transmutes itself. Considered by the ancients to be the most perfect symbolic form of pure *psyche* in nature, the chrysalis demonstrates the transformative power of combining self-discipline and freedom in order to release the angelic being of divine beauty, symmetry and grace.

This hexagram is paired with its complement, 33, NECESSITY.

Hexagram Sequence

After things have been tempered, they can never be broken:
METAMORPHOSIS is crystalizing the invisible.

Beings do not rise above themselves unless the potential already exists within their essence. Because that potential already exists within its nature, its full realization is part of its natural growth and requires no special striving in order to attain it. Striving, instead, pulls the being off its individual *tao* and into a realm of artificial complexities of thought, desire and intent. The potential for self-transcendence, in other words, is invisible, imperceptible to the five senses—fully realizing that potential is called *crystalizing the invisible*. It is, nonetheless, a *presence*, a *felt longing* that pulls the soul into a period of incubation, wherein that secret potential can be worked upon by the natural incitement and energy of the visible *awaiting transformation*. The deathless awakens itself, departs the chrysalis.

Mantic Formula

The bubble bursts and inside and outside are no more:
You become light incarnate.

The soul in the World Soul. The air inside a bubble and the air outside a bubble. The bubble bursts and inside and outside are reunited—they are no different, they are no different before the membrane ends. The perfection of the symbol of the bubble—the perfection of the manner in which it articulates *Truth*—is startling when witnessed in the mirror of *psychic substance*. It gives miraculous form to the ancients' wisdom saying, *There is no inside nor outside*. There is just the one undifferentiated *substance*. Only the soul can hold both the *One* and the *Many* in awareness at the same time, experiencing the *One* individuating within each of the *Many*. Essence recognizes essence: the *One* recognizes its immortal self within each of its mortal forms. The caterpillar eating a leaf recognizes the butterfly drifting by—the soul senses the presence of its metamorphic potential as though it were an angel drifting by. As a whole, this formula signifies that you feel the material form slipping away until all that remains is the universal symbol of metamorphosis: a sphere of transparent light drifting by.

INTENT

Bottom Line. Dawn archer: Free of rider and horses, the chariot circles the star clock.

Second Line. Dawn archer: The Magi sleeping at the bottom of the well of stars.

Third Line. Dawn archer: The blacksmith midwifes the pregnant stone.

Fourth Line. Dawn archer: Thunder singing the secret songs of ascension.

Fifth Line. Dawn archer: Original time flows from the springs of the sea.

Top Line. Dawn archer: The gods kindle a polar fire to ignite new stars.

31

TRANSCENDENCE

OUTER NATURE:	MOON
INNER NATURE:	LIGHTNING

Lightning within, Moon without: Motivation within, Completion without

Moon outside symbolizes completion, while Lightning inside symbolizes inspiration. Not all symbols are archetypes but all archetypes are symbols—images that carry the direct meaning given them in their divine origination. Their meaning—their value—cannot be divorced from the *presence* of the Divine Heart of their birth: they are eternally present, *living messengers* bearing their divine messages across All Creation. Because they are born of Divine Love, all these living messengers are called *Angels*—it is irrelevant whether their individual messages are *light* or *dark*, as all are born of the same origin and to think of some as *angelic* and others *demonic* reduces understanding of the sacred nature of each and limits the soul's participation in their world of pre-manifestation. The World Soul, then, is the homeland of *Completion*, the already-prepared realm of freedom for those who make of their own heart a mirror of the Divine Heart—and of their own symbolic nature a winged flight back to origination.

This hexagram is paired with its complement, 32, EXPERIENCE.

HEXAGRAM SEQUENCE

After things have transformed, they are utterly transparent:
TRANSCENDENCE is the visible returning to the invisible.

The metamorphosed soul paves the way for the body in the world of manifestation. For the uninitiated, the body suffers greatly from the *instinct to transcend*—it keeps their attention pointed elsewhere than the manifest world they inhabit, ensuring they are at home in neither realm. For the initiated, the *instinct to transcend* is a beckoning to transcend not the world, but the self. Consciously or unconsciously, the body identifies with some symbol it has come across in the course of its life and, in this way, its self and the symbol become fused as an ego-identity: it is this symbol, therefore, that is the true object of the *instinct to transcend*. The soul stands in immediate contrast to that symbol, utterly transparent, utterly empty of attachment to *staying* or *going*. The soul already stands on the other side of metamorphosis, beckoning to the body: it is the body, then, that awakens to its own transpersonal essence—transcending the symbol-self, the body naturally and spontaneously assumes the manifest form of the soul. This calling forth by the soul of the body is like the hen calling the hatchling to break out of the egg: what had been invisible is suddenly the real world.

MANTIC FORMULA

The moon concentrates the sun's light into a single lightning bolt:
You cannot help setting the night sky ablaze.

To be a soul is to be seen by other souls. To see other souls as image-symbols is to be seen as an image-symbol by other souls. The individuation of the *One* into its infinite *Pure Ideas* seals, in turn, the image-symbol that *is* each immortal soul. To transcend one's individual soul is to fulfill the absolute meaning and value of one's symbol, to bring it to full realization in order to complete its *journey back* to the source of divine inspiration: this *reading* of one's own symbol is the act that initiates *transcendence*, transporting the soul into the realm of *Pure Idea*, wherein it awakens to its own revelatory nature as an utterly free and independent *expression* of the *Divine Heart*. It is this *revelatory expression of original divine meaning* that marks the transcendence of the symbol-soul into the living archetype. As a whole, this formula signifies that you take your place among the suns of the eternal constellations.

INTENT

Bottom Line. Arrow star: Lilith drinking at the confluence of all rivers in the celestial spring.

Second Line. Arrow star: The lightning-dragon hatches from the moon-pearl.

Third Line. Arrow star: The plumb bob hangs true to centering the pole star.

Fourth Line. Arrow star: The hidden ocean surveys the first creation.

Fifth Line. Arrow star: Eternity flows from the mother of the sky.

Top Line. Arrow star: The archangels cast into the heavens as constellations.

32

EXPERIENCE

OUTER NATURE:	SUN
INNER NATURE:	WIND

Wind within, Sun without: Adaptation within, Creation without

Sun outside symbolizes creative force, while Wind inside symbolizes adaptive power. When the Work is completed, the Work begins anew. When the blacksmith's forge crowns the *Glory*, then Divine Fire has indeed descended into the Bellows, raking the coals of Gold to pitch black until, distilled of all dross, Silver Water turns the tides backward into the Shining Abyss: ascending another cycle on the spiral is only possible by descending another cycle on the spiral. Full realization of one's angelic nature is the natural and spontaneous evolution of the soul—it is the precursor to bringing *psychic substance* to bear on the ills and promises of the world of manifestation.

This hexagram is paired with its complement, 31, TRANSCENDENCE.

Hexagram Sequence

After things have entered the celestial, they reenter the world:
EXPERIENCE is the invisible returning to the visible.

Coming back into the human realm is like the wind coursing everywhere under the sun without barriers: it is the soul's freedom to return as it desires, to enter into circumstances it wishes to explore, to pour out its love for life from an open heart, that makes this such a meaningful encounter with nature and other people. The uninitiated do not appreciate the depth of feelings welling up within such individuals, whose experience is that of an adventurer set loose on an unknown continent with all the skills and resources needed to thrive. For the initiated soul, the quest is for new experiences, new first-hand encounters with spirit, human nature and nature—it opens up new vistas of opportunities and proves to be a receptive time for starting new endeavors or adapting old ones to new circumstances. Such an individual lacks caution but does not move too soon, has the utmost patience but does not move too late: it is as if they are perfectly attuned to the timing of things, arriving at the foreordained turning point to add their energy to the direction and momentum of change. What they bring back from the invisible adds to the wellbeing of the visible. As the ancients' wisdom teachings have long sought to light the path: *The Way of the Initiated is to Unite Heaven and Earth!*

Mantic Formula

Time passes:
You walk in place.

The wise soul finds its way to an endeavor perfectly suited to its nature. Individuals who settle into such situations discover there exists real room for their creative energies and past experiences to merge into a lifeway of unexpected potential and personal fulfillment. For the soul, this is a *deepening* of the experience of human nature, while for the body, it is the acquisition of a level of understanding and skills much greater than ever imagined. Each new set of challenges offers greater opportunity to actually bring the celestial into the visible—to *apply* the experiences in the World Soul to one's roles and responsibilities in the world of manifestations. To *demonstrate* the efficacy of the law of spiritual cause-and-effect within the World Body, to manifest the nature of the initiated soul within the historical era of one's lifetime, and to do so with humility, empathy and grace—this is the reason one takes up the kind of *service* to other beings that unites heaven and earth within oneself. As a whole, this formula signifies that you stay with this endeavor of service, perfecting the work while cultivating your own nature—looking neither to advance or withdraw—for a long cycle of time.

INTENT

Bottom Line. Night crossing: The ancient gods and goddesses dwelling in the one eternal year.

Second Line. Solstice crossing: The sky celebrates the one born at the right time.

Third Line. Comet crossing: The child of the waters grows new antlers every Spring.

Fourth Line. Ferry crossing: The river Lethe flows backward into unforgetfulness.

Fifth Line. Phoenix crossing: The mirror sets itself afire to rise from its own ashes.

Top Line. Day crossing: The three fires as one in the sacrificial service.

33

NECESSITY

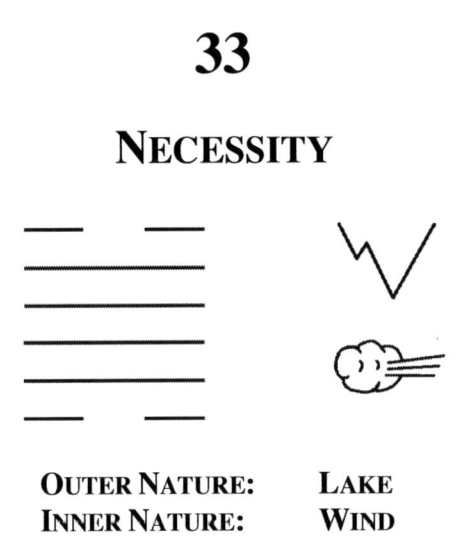

OUTER NATURE: **LAKE**
INNER NATURE: **WIND**

Wind within, Lake without: Adaptation within, Wonder without

Lake outside symbolizes communion with nature, human nature and spirit, while Wind inside symbolizes patient resolution of obstructions. Taking stock of the ills befallen the world of manifestation, the soul depends on the sense of *the inevitable* for guidance. The initiated, empowered by their vision of perfect harmony and balance emanating from the Divine Heart of the *One*, do not shrink from addressing matters that cannot be walked away from. The work laid out for the initiated during this transition between Ages necessitates curing the twin sicknesses of the *desecration of nature* and the *desecration of human nature*.

This hexagram is paired with its complement, 30, METAMORPHOSIS.

Hexagram Sequence

After things have taken root, they follow the seasons:
Necessity is aligning with the inevitable.

There exist many rationalizations for acting in opposition to *The Good* but they are all negated by their common denominator: self-destruction. This terrible trait exhibits the results of the soul-crushing social conditioning of the modern mind, which turns against itself in a deep-seated sense of unworthiness and self-loathing. The initiated view all this with compassionate equanimity as the sorrowful price paid for passing through the Age of Darkness, the long winter of which is finally turning. Though the soul's attention is called to the necessary remedies of the manifest world's ills, successful remedies are found only against the background awareness of the *Battle for the World Soul*: action can and must take place by participating in the social structures of understanding and influence, but those efforts come to naught if they are isolated from the wider sense of *intentional crisis* within the World Soul. The original Act of Creation establishes an oceanic realm of *psychic substance* predisposed to peaceful coexistence and mutual regard—but *psychic substance* is formed by *intent* and intent is formed by *character*. The character of *psyche* itself, its nature, its essence, its inclination toward *The Good* or not, is generally a long-standing feeling with which the soul identifies and does not question. It is as if there was a world of absolute peace among people and harmony with nature, when suddenly, a small group of people discovered metal-working and descended on their neighbors with bloody swords, subjecting them to untold horrors. In terror, these innocents sought self-defense by discovering the art of sword-making and, in the process, the art of war. Within the World Soul, this metaphor stands for the schism created by the forces of the counter-Creation and the contagion of fear they engender.

Mantic Formula

What survives looks back from the end:
You follow the only possible path.

From within the timelessness of the World Soul, the eventual outcome of the desecration of *The Good* stands like a monument to the *failure of will*. A new alliance forms around avoiding this end—one dedicated to healing the wound in the World Soul and its resultant manifestation of restoration within the World Body. Within the world of manifestation, the only inevitable end that avoids self-destruction is the new World Age, the *Golden Age of Humanity*, wherein All benefit from its reign of *universal peace and prospering*. As a whole, this formula signifies that you are guided from within to restore balance and harmony to the manifest world, regardless of the obstacles and personal discomforts.

INTENT

Bottom Line. Destined omen: The sun-rope tied to the hitching post of the mountaintop.

Second Line. Destined accord: Angels and humankind drink from the well of ambrosia.

Third Line. Destined character: Wind and rain sculpting a balancing rock.

Fourth Line. Destined reversal: Shadow souls undergo the inevitable change of heart.

Fifth Line. Destined fortitude: The earth lion provides mother's milk for the heavens.

Top Line. Destined key: The spirit serpent sheds its skin every day.

34

Reflecting

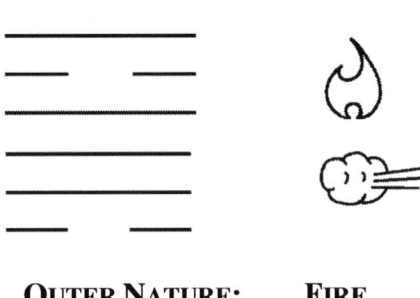

Outer Nature: Fire
Inner Nature: Wind

Wind within, Fire without: Adaptation within, Knowledge without

Fire outside symbolizes knowledge, while Wind inside symbolizes adaptation. Nature is the epitome of *adaptation*. Intelligence is the epitome of *knowledge*. The greater part of the ancients' wisdom is handed down in the teaching, *Everything is connected, and It has intelligence*. Everything in the natural world is interrelated and that whole has intelligent awareness. That whole which has intelligent awareness is alive. This living being made up of all the parts of infinite Nature has thought. This thinking, living being is the mother of all things. That which gives rise to the mother of all things is invisible. These two, the visible and the invisible, mirror one another: just as the leaves of trees mark the existence of the invisible wind, all of Nature marks the existence of the invisible. That which has existence and is invisible is Spirit. To know Nature intimately is to know Spirit intimately. To love Nature is to be loved by Nature. To love Spirit is to be loved by Spirit. Nature adapts to the will of Spirit. Intelligence thinks in images. Images are the *appearance* of the invisible, the *knowing* of the invisible. The will of Spirit speaks in images. Nature takes the form of Spirit's images.

This hexagram is paired with its complement, 29, Resolve.

Hexagram Sequence

After things have attuned to the Already, they are guided from within:
Reflecting is wisdom beyond inner and outer.

The *Already* is that which one finds upon incarnating. Attuning to the already-existing is *spiritual adaptation*. Participating in the already-existing is *spiritual knowledge*. Ever mindful of their immortal nature, the initiated enter the mortal realm with the express purpose of manifesting the timeless truths of the ancient gods and goddesses within the historical era into which they are born. Spiritual adaptation, then, extends to the need to adapt the timeless truths to the timebound social, cultural and historical customs in which souls find themselves. Spiritual knowledge, likewise, extends to understanding how to apply the ancients' wisdom teachings to the modern lifeway. The uninitiated fall prey to the siren song of *need*: convinced from an early age of their dependence on others for their fulfillment, people search everywhere for what they are *missing*—affection, recognition, gratification, dominance, subjection, and all the other *needs* that destroy a person's sense of autonomy. The initiated participate in life but do not become attached to things or people in such a way that they lose their bearings in the mortal world—they maintain their angelic nature, sharing their measure of the Divine Heart with all, while exploring the world of manifestation to the fullest.

Mantic Formula

The soul throws one forward:
You drink the nectar of spring blossoms.

To enter the realm of manifestation is to encounter human nature first and nature second. To a great extent, one's exposure to human nature colors one's experience of nature, at least at the beginning. But there comes a time in one's life when one's conscious awareness of nature has the opportunity to cast off all preconceptions and encounter the presence of the spirit within nature as a living relationship—one's body responds to the World Body as one's soul does to being part of the World Soul. The sudden breakthrough into recognition of the living intelligence of nature and the inability of the world to adapt benignly to continued desecration marks a profound mental and emotional shift in the degree of one's concern for all life. Breaking free of all past explanations, descriptions and justifications regarding human nature's relationship with nature, one takes up advocacy for a return to a balanced lifeway in harmony with the entirety of nature. The uninitiated may take this opportunity to indulge in righteous indignation and zealotry, the short-term gains of which might seem justifiable, but in the long-term alienates potential allies and sets up new obstacles. The initiated do not act in a way that creates new backlashes that run counter to their intended purpose—they see themselves, rather, as the living manifestation of an alliance of souls working in the pre-manifestation realm to secure the eternal wellbeing of nature and human nature, both. As a whole, this formula signifies that you are blessed and loved by Nature as one of Its own.

INTENT

Bottom Line. Ethereal theater: The unavoidable disaster is avoided.

Second Line. Ethereal gathering: Past star, past wolf, past orchid, past lives.

Third Line. Ethereal egg: The sun casts no shadow.

Fourth Line. Ethereal shelter: Nonresistance is the best defense.

Fifth Line. Ethereal gold: The image cannot be held by mirror, water or eye.

Top Line. Ethereal roots: The panacea changes the imagination of humankind.

35

PROPAGATION

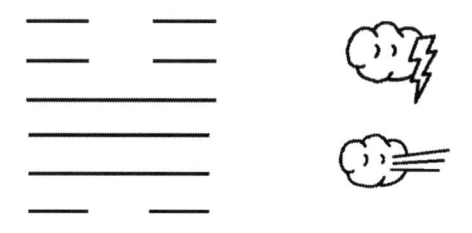

OUTER NATURE:	LIGHTNING
INNER NATURE:	WIND

Wind within, Lightning without: Adaptation within, Motivation without

Lightning outside symbolizes surprise, while Wind inside symbolizes permeation. When the initiated take up work in the manifestation realm, they inevitably attract the attention of others of high potential. This presents an opportunity to propagate the wisdom teachings of the ancients but, like all opportunities, carries with it the possibility of missteps. The humility and self-deprecation of the initiated is well-established, yet there are too many instances of even the well-trained losing their bearings and imagining that the focus of attention was upon the teacher and not the teachings—such efforts inevitably fail and, worse, lead others off the path. The traditional path is based upon the elements Lightning and Wind: the teachings use *surprise* to break up the stagnation of fixed habits of mind and *permeation* to pass through the personality in order to address the soul directly.

This hexagram is paired with its complement, 28, RESTORATION.

HEXAGRAM SEQUENCE

After things have found their place, they set others above them:
PROPAGATION is the fostering of the teachings, not the teacher.

Lightning is *sudden*, Wind is *gradual*: the traditional teachings follow two strategies—*sudden*, which aims for a rapid breakthrough, and *gradual*, which implements a longer path of self-cultivation as preparation for the breakthrough. *Sudden* is utilized for those whose many lifetimes have prepared them for an easy and straight-forward *remembering* of the teachings from previous incarnations. *Gradual* is for earnest and sincere souls willing to dedicate many years to self-liberation. From the larger perspective, however, *sudden* and *gradual* are the same approach, since even after breakthrough, it is necessary to spend years in self-cultivation. There is no room for personal advancement for a true teacher—their sole focus is the advancement of their student. Though it may appear otherwise, the true teacher is, in every essential way, the student's servant—it takes great dedication and concern to help the student find their source of *motivation* and expose them to the relevance of the ancient teachings to the historical era. As the ancients were fond of saying, *It is difficult to find a true teacher, but it is many times more difficult to find a true student.*

MANTIC FORMULA

The closer to the light, the greater the shadow cast:
Your shadow engulfs all Creation.

Where is the field within which the ancients' teachings are propagated? Within the soul. Those who share the teachings with others do so out of a sense of repaying the debt of their own initiation. But that takes nothing away from the fact that the ground of propagation is within the soul: the source of initiates' humility and self-deprecation is their full awareness that there is never any end to further realization of the wisdom of the ancients—only by continually perfecting their *perception* and *interpretation* of the living elements of All Creation do they increase the scope and meaning lodged within the image-symbols of the manifestation and pre-manifestation realms. The initiated utilize the Wind of *permeation* to interpenetrate the divine origin of each symbol's meaning, which ever results in unexpectedly experiencing the Lightning of *surprise* as rapidly expanding *understanding* blossoms and sends forth wind-blown seeds into the wild and untilled lands of the World Soul. Wisdom grows because it grows within the individual. Wisdom does not just mean understanding or intelligence or even correct action—it means an immediate and intuitive grasp of the relationships between things, between their essences, that guides one to act in accord with the *One* at the right time in the right place with the right intention. As a whole, this formula signifies that your wisdom stands so close to the Divine Fire, that your experience of the Unknown, of the Great Mystery, holds All Creation within cupped hands.

INTENT

Bottom Line. Nameless seed: Nature protects humankind at great cost to itself.

Second Line. Nameless trunk: Indomitable strength of purpose within.

Third Line. Nameless branches: Infinite teachers, one teaching.

Fourth Line. Nameless flower: The teachers' teacher.

Fifth Line. Nameless fruit: The goddess of wisdom calls forth musical scales.

Top Line. Nameless seed: Humankind protects nature at great cost to itself.

36

RESILIENCE

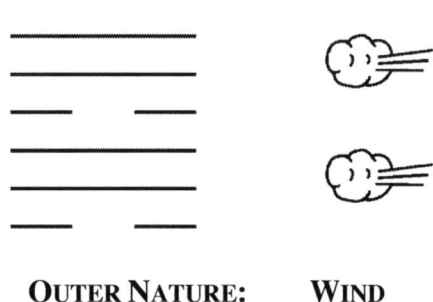

OUTER NATURE: WIND
INNER NATURE: WIND

Wind within, Wind without: Adaptation within, Adaptation without

Wind outside symbolizes patient resolution, while Wind inside symbolizes patient resolution. Spirit moves like the wind. It penetrates into and through the least openings and fills the entire sky with its presence. It can stroke an infant's cheek with the gentlest breeze and it can drive a shaft of straw through a fencepost. Wind is everywhere, all the time, touching all things in the manifestation world: but it is not until it enters the living being and becomes *breath* that it is a *soul*. Spirit is everywhere, all the time, touching all things in the pre-manifestation world: but it is not until it coalesces around an individual identity—an individual *intent*—that it is a *soul*. The interpenetration of spirit and soul is part of the Great Mystery of Creation: it is like the roots of the tree interpenetrating the soil of the world itself—the soil enters the roots and nurtures them, while the roots penetrate the soil and take hold. Spirit provides soul a world to live in, so the two are not easily distinguished—how, then, is it that an individual intent arises to form a unique identity within universal spirit? As with the soil and the root, the answer is, *With a seed*. The seed of the soul is an image-symbol sown into the soil of spirit as a *living message* cast into the infinite by the *One*. This living image falls like a seed into the soil of spirit—into the *psychic substance*—of the World Soul in an act wherein *symbol-making* and *soul-making* are identical. This, then, points directly to the *moment of initiation*, when the soul first grasps its own origin and destination as a living symbol of Divine Thought—a moment, however stumbled upon accidentally, that forever separates the initiated and uninitiated.

This hexagram is paired with its complement, 27, DARING.

Hexagram Sequence

After things have embodied humility, they are at their most pliable:
RESILIENCE is the indomitable spirit of perfect tempering.

Intellectual brilliance does not help—it is, in fact, a hindrance. Cleverness with words only digs the hole deeper. Mimicry and imitation crack and fall away at the first challenge. Intuition serves well enough but can be side-tracked by fascination. Simple compliance produces only literal understandings. But the heart—the center of deep-seated resonances that defy logic and abandon conventional wisdom—the heart: essence recognizes essence, like a bell singing softly when another is stuck, like pitch perfect harmony between two strangers from different lands, essence expands and contracts, like the tide, touching other essences and being touched by other essences. When *heart* is understood to be the *soul*, the seat of feelings far beyond the range of human emotions, then *what is it that resonates* becomes a matter of import: the medium within which souls dwell is spirit, *psychic substance*, so it is this medium that transfers the resonant sensations between souls. But what medium transfers the resonance between oneself and one's symbol? What is the medium of self-recognition? *Language*. Not the language of Earth, not the language of the manifestation realm, but the original language, the angelic language, *The Word* of immanent Divine Thought, the language of pre-manifestation, in which the *Pure Idea* emanates into its infinite meanings within its image—no less visceral than a mystic talisman bearing a unique symbol struck from the forge of the archangels. It is in this *language of origin* that soul-making and symbol-making occur simultaneously, creating the *memory* of their *arising-together*. This memory of the language of origin is *anamnesis*, the soul's recollection of all past lives writ in its signal symbol.

The perfectly tempered sword has both strength and flexibility. The perfectly tempered soul recovers from, and adjusts easily to, shock, misfortune and change. The perfectly tempered sword undergoes repeated heating and cooling. The perfectly tempered soul undergoes repeated fluctuations in good fortune and misfortune. Intellect, cleverness, imitation, intuition or compliance—none of these carry one through all the way to the moment of initiation. Patient resolution of emotional doubts and mental habits—this is the path of the indomitable spirit, the *mystic sword* cutting through all illusions, that carries one to its eventual end in the Completion of the Work.

Mantic Formula

Paradise beckons:
You can see it from where you stand.

Spirit moves like the wind. Awareness moves with spirit. Spirit carries awareness. Awareness directs spirit. These two are called *spirit awareness* and *spirit wind*. The initiated engage in shamanic flight: within the spirit world, spirit awareness directs spirit wind to the land of peace and prospering for all. It is all within reach of a single exhale. In the world of manifestation, spirit wind is *faith*—not blind faith in what one is told, but irrefutable faith in what one has personally experienced. There exist fated moments where irrefutable faith intersects anamnesis—those of high discernment find this new path is the shortcut to the Completion of the Work. As a whole, this formula signifies that you succeed because you possess *Infinite Patience*.

Intent

Bottom Line. Buoyant reserve: The sun burns inside dreaming dewdrops.

Second Line. Buoyant reserve: The windmill of fire turns age upon age.

Third Line. Buoyant reserve: The gods are stars and divine tricksters.

Fourth Line. Buoyant reserve: Living light is collected in memory wells.

Fifth Line. Buoyant reserve: The world tree encircles the starry sky.

Top Line. Buoyant reserve: The riverbed returns to its ancient course.

37

POTENTIALITY

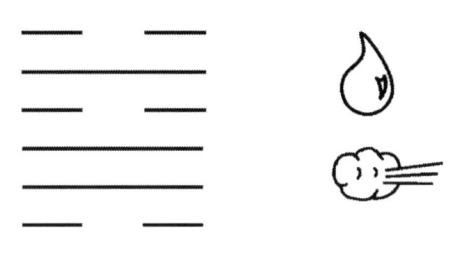

OUTER NATURE: **WATER**
INNER NATURE: **WIND**

Wind within, Water without: Adaptation within, Mystery without

Water outside symbolizes the Great Mystery, while Wind inside symbolizes patient resolution. *Outside* means that which is beyond the limits of the soul's awareness. The Great Mystery is the unfathomable and inexplicable reality of Creation. Whether speaking of the visible or the invisible Creation, it is, first and foremost, the vastness of its scope, the sheer enormity of its compass, that sets a limit on what can be known. Contrariwise, investigating the reaches of its smallest parts opens up a realm of equally unapproachable dimension. Awareness is faced on all sides by *The Already Existing* Creation that is neither a human universe nor one created by souls. Grandeur and greater grandeur at every turn: there is no end to the possible forms that Nature and Spirit might take in their adaptation to the Great Mystery.

This hexagram is paired with its complement, 26, ENNOBLING.

HEXAGRAM SEQUENCE

After things have acquired potency, they have resources to spare:
POTENTIALITY is the diversification of the sacred.

The primordial Act of Creation begins as a state of potentiality that builds until it crosses the threshold of actualization and becomes reality. This first act of origination establishes the structure for all acts of creation that follow. The Great Mystery borders All, offering up the entirety of its *Plentitude of Possibility* to the ancient gods and goddesses that they might accept it, imbuing it with their own sacred essence and scattering the seeds to the ten directions. This has forever after been called, *The art of harnessing the Great Mystery*. The *living potential* of The Unknown surrounds every act of creation, infusing it with an unpredictable element of augmentation due to the synergism introduced by The Unknown. This *added value* of the augmentation cannot be assessed ahead of time but allocates, in every instance, more meaning than appears possible, given the sum of its makings. *Potentiality*, from this perspective, appears as *the Imagination of the One*.

MANTIC FORMULA

The oasis shimmers in the moonlight:
You drink a toast with ancient wayfarers.

The art of harnessing the Great Mystery does not involve conceiving something to create and then, in some manner, mixing it with the Great Mystery. It involves, rather, constantly dwelling in—or, at the least, on the border of—the Great Mystery: it means training oneself to remain in the numinous presence of the otherworldly, to sense the immediacy of the infinite possibilities set to pour into each moment. Within the pre-manifestation realm of the World Soul, *harnessing the Great Mystery* points to the soul's evocation of the *living potential* of the Great Mystery, manifested as the intent to open up the oceanic *psychic substance* to the unforeseeable possibilities the Great Mystery offers up *in response* to an articulated *need*. The initiated, in other words, determine places where unmet needs exist, translate those into image-symbols and project them into the Great Mystery, taking great care to invest those image-symbols with the emotional significance appropriate to the need-at-hand. As a whole, this formula signifies that you do not fall prey to the mirage of limitation and deficiency but, rather, celebrate the truth of plentitude in the company of other old souls.

INTENT

Bottom Line. Temple celestial: Poured earth invokes the spirit of flourishing.

Second Line. Temple celestial: The treasure house spills open its universe of good.

Third Line. Temple celestial: Fathoming the depth of the sea with a ladle.

Fourth Line. Temple celestial: Only the sacred ritual of self-sacrifice opens the gate of initiation.

Fifth Line. Temple celestial: In the wake of the final naming, Ouroboros names the first.

Top Line. Temple celestial: Time, reined and wheeled, worships only the charioteer.

38

PROTECTING

OUTER NATURE:	MOUNTAIN
INNER NATURE:	WIND

Wind within, Mountain without: Adaptation within, Incubation without

Mountain outside symbolizes interruption, while Wind inside symbolizes adaptation. Wind, adaptation, signifies life and, therefore, both nature and human nature. In particular, it relates to the specific path of adaptation they are taking. Mountain, interruption, signifies the need to stop the direction of their adaptation in order to effect a momentous change of course. If further adaptation of nature and human nature is to be had, then it must be based upon widespread agreement that everything is sacred. This universal acknowledgement is the sacralization of all things that, alone, is able to halt the modern mind's desecration of nature and human nature.

This hexagram is paired with its complement, 25, ALLIANCE.

Hexagram Sequence

After things have expanded, they must consolidate:
Protecting is revering what cannot be replaced.

The potentiality for change is infinite. The will to change is finite. Following the natural cycles of growth and decay, civilization can endure forever; ignoring them is the root of self-destruction. Expansion cannot go on forever—it must obey the cycle of the seasons: growth must periodically be halted and actually reversed in order to consolidate the gains made. This period of consolidation must be internalized, as well, so that there exists the opportunity to reevaluate goals, priorities and the best means to the most beneficial ends. Stopping and consolidating is Mountain, which signifies stillness, contemplation and meditation. Going forward patiently is Wind, which signifies appropriate adaptation to circumstances as they change. There is no excuse for not avoiding avoidable disaster—Autumn and Winter arrive every cycle, providing amble opportunity to prepare. In the world of manifestation, the question must be one of *values*: what cannot be replaced? what must be protected? what angelic properties of human nature are at risk of being lost? what divine aspects of the natural world are threatened by human nature?

Mantic Formula

Water nurtures all it touches:
You spread your branches wide.

The intent to protect arises from love. The soul loves because it is loved. It is cared for, provided for, as a fish in the sea—all of Creation is a loving embrace, a constant reminder of the *enveloping reverence* in which every soul is held. Younger souls do not sense this immediately, mistaking the plentitude of Creation for an impersonal storehouse, but older souls, with a long line of lifetimes behind them, know the love, care and concern of the Whole for its every Part. As the soul grows to reciprocate the love it is shown, so too does it grow to seek to protect that which gifts it such protection. Of course, it is not the Whole which the soul seeks to safeguard, but those Parts in the most vulnerable conditions in the world of manifestation. It is appreciation for the frailty of the manifestations and how easily they can be lost forever—and the gratitude and reverence for that which has bestowed the soul's immortality—that drive the initiated to halt further expansion and establish a period of consolidation during which all facets of the relationship between nature and human nature are reconsidered and corrected where need be. The finite will to change rises to meet the challenge by forming a tidal wave of allies, joined by renewed faith in a vision of the Golden Age of Humanity. As a whole, this formula signifies that your love and reverence for All Life transforms the imagination of the uninitiated.

INTENT

Bottom Line. Phoenix ambrosia: The yoked spirit-oxen till the night.

Second Line. Phoenix ambrosia: The sky-shadow dissolves all at once.

Third Line. Phoenix ambrosia: Living light finding its origin.

Fourth Line. Phoenix ambrosia: Mystics breaking the trance state and journeying the spirit world.

Fifth Line. Phoenix ambrosia: The constellations still walk the earth and perplex fate.

Top Line. Phoenix ambrosia: The watershed of souls empties out into the Eternal Sea of Love.

39

INDIVIDUALITY

OUTER NATURE:	MOON
INNER NATURE:	WIND

Wind within, Moon without: Adaptation within, Completion without

Moon outside symbolizes completion of a cycle, while Wind inside symbolizes adaptation. The quiet. The owl hoot floats across the meadow beneath a full moon. The stillness, timeless. The constellations, the campfires of the ancestors watching over their descendants. A lone figure standing against the sea of stars. *Nearly Home*. Light streams from every pore. *Waiting for the tide*. It is the first person to stand, shadow in hand, and address the Universe directly. *We Are I Am*. A ghost floats like an owl through the mists. Millennia pass. One by one, each makes it here. And each is the first.

This hexagram is paired with its complement, 24, FOUNDING.

Hexagram Sequence

After things have sensed divinity in others, they sense their own:
INDIVIDUALITY is an Idea in the One Mind.

It is easier to stare into one's own shadow than to stare into one's own light. The dark, human nature is accustomed to. The back of the cave, huddled against the spirits of the night. The awful nightmares visited upon children young and old. One's own shadow only holds so many terrors, most already hinted at in dreams, if not lived out in waking horrors. But one's own light. One's own angelic nature. One's higher soul. That is awe-full, like staring unblinking into the sun. Blinding. To stare unblinking into *The Good*. Into the eyes of *Pure Light*, staring unblinking back into the depths of one's soul, past every sorrow, shame, resentment, wrong-doing, and evil thought: illuminating every corner, casting out every life-negating shadow, evaporating every self-destructive habit of thought, emotion or memory—*Pure Light*, the power of which would be terrifying if not accompanied by the force of *Pure Love* in equal measure. This, then, is the birth of the true individual: the lower soul recognizes that the conditioned self, the ego identity, needs to die in order for the true individual to be reborn. To engage one's own angelic nature is to stare unblinking into the sun. The conditioned identity burns away like a morning mist—all that remains is sunlight on clear air: the unconditioned self, the higher soul, emerges from past ages, unaware of the time passed, and unites with the lower soul. It is out of this union that the true individual is born: a lone figure standing against the sea of stars.

Mantic Formula

Among all the stars in the sky, only one sun:
You are a crossroads of memory and understanding.

The *immortal spirit body* arises from this union of the higher soul and lower soul. It is the two of them joined as one, yet it is one, blossoming forth from the roots and branches of the two. The true individual becomes divine because the *immortal spirit body* spontaneously returns the two to the *One*, whose divinity is *transmitted soul-to-soul* from the *One* to the individualized *Many*. As a whole, this formula signifies that you unite the lower soul of memory and the higher soul of understanding into a single new soul of eternal freedom.

INTENT

Bottom Line. Obsidian mirror: Smoke from nature's battle cry reaches the heavens.

Second Line. Obsidian mirror: Iron-words feather-symbols make.

Third Line. Obsidian mirror: Sun and moon cannot a more perfect child conceive.

Fourth Line. Obsidian mirror: An infinitude of roads but only one home.

Fifth Line. Obsidian mirror: The angel of oaks still puts forth all the acorns in the world.

Top Line. Obsidian mirror: A land without words produces prophets without end.

40

DEESCALATING

OUTER NATURE:	SUN
INNER NATURE:	WATER

Water within, Sun without: Mystery within, Creation without

Sun outside symbolizes creative daring, while Water inside symbolizes one's own mysterious nature. Just as periods of expansion are followed by periods of contraction, periods of intensification are followed by periods of deescalation. Times of heightened self-awareness and spiritual advance are like great bonfires that impassion the soul and inflame the imagination. This awakens both a greater sense of capacity to accomplish significant deeds and a greater sense of responsibility to fulfill one's sacred duty. It is at this exact point that the initiated turn their attention back to the *shadow* and all the *hidden* it holds. Water is the symbol of mystery and inner mystery draws one back into one's own unfathomable nature—one's own *shadow*—but now in the sense of the inner abyss providing a dwelling place for all the *not-yet-created* awaiting birth. This is not a matter of remembering potentiality but, rather, of remembering that one's own mysterious nature is a tunnel, so to speak, to the vast *inner earth*, wherein dwell images not even the angels have dreamed. One does not arrive at this point by accident nor until the previous work is done— but at the height of personal power, the furnace must be tamped down: spiritual energy that seeks to leap into action and explore must first be moderated by sinking back into the *creative shadow*, the depths of the world of manifestation *mirroring back* its chthonic reflections of the World Soul's images.

This hexagram is paired with its complement, 23, NONINTERFERENCE.

HEXAGRAM SEQUENCE

After things have recognized uniqueness, they must recognize equality:
DEESCALATING is the hidden treasure of mutual benefit.

The initiated voluntarily let die the shadow self of the acquired ego-identity. They do not let die the *creative shadow* making up the larger part of the lower soul's *memory,* or *anamnesis.* This is the constructive, life-affirming, shadow of the lower soul—the part that longs for reunion with the higher soul. Creative as it is, life-affirming as it is, it is still *shadow* because it is impenetrable to conscious inquiry or investigation—personal though it is, it is barely so, being the individual's umbilical cord to the *ancestral memory* of nature and, therefore, human nature. Like a fortress impervious to attack or siege, it lowers its drawbridge only to release its symbols of long-forgotten living matter. Rather than accelerate forward out of strength and enthusiasm, the *immortal spirit body* holds close, slows down, pulls back and waits: further progress is not the imperative; listening, taking in, incorporating, embodying, and giving expression to—this honoring of the uncounted generations of lifetimes and lifeforms that lead up to the living manifestations is what makes it possible for the *immortal spirit body* to carry this primordial creative material back to the *One* and, in that pilgrimage of return, enrich the spiritual imagery of the world of pre-manifestation.

MANTIC FORMULA

Strange shadows eclipse the daystar:
You shine like the new moon.

Some souls shine brightly, some souls shine darkly. The distinction has nothing to do with better or worse, or good or evil, but, instead, with the degree to which one identifies with and gives voice to the Great Mystery. Those who shine darkly hold the *mystery of mortality* especially dear, revering the unimaginable image-symbols generated not by the archangels of the *Pure Idea* realm, but by the stone and bone and stars and ichor of the ancient gods and goddesses of living death. Remembrance of the dead—and the uncountable moments of passing from life into death through the *Gate of Dying*—is the moment-by-moment ritual of the *immortal spirit body* celebrating the *eternal mortal* it carries with it back to the *One*. As a whole, this formula signifies that you do not turn away from the shadow of mortality but embrace it as the living mystery of the light shining in the very depths of the underworld.

INTENT

Bottom Line. Mutual surrender: Giants of molten stone emerge from their caves to receive offerings.

Second Line. Mutual surrender: A generation of humankind incapable of violent thought, word or act.

Third Line. Mutual surrender: A warlord defeated by a peacemaker.

Fourth Line. Mutual surrender: Musicians singing songs of longing and metamorphosis.

Fifth Line. Mutual surrender: Forgotten gods and nameless goddesses pantomiming wordless hymns.

Top Line. Mutual surrender: An Age of Peace between the Angel of Earth and the Angel of Humankind.

41

CONTENTMENT

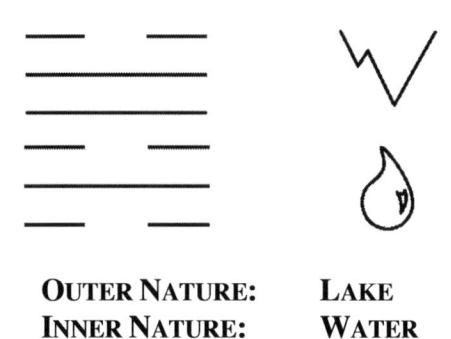

OUTER NATURE: **LAKE**
INNER NATURE: **WATER**

Water within, Lake without: Mystery within, Wonder without

Lake outside symbolizes happiness, communion, while Water inside symbolizes one's own mysterious nature. The image is that of hidden water beneath a lake, signifying an inexhaustible source of wellbeing for all—no matter how many come to drink from the lake, it is replenished from below. This represents a period of enthusiastic energy to be shared with others of like heart-mind—a period fueled in large part by the dreams, accidents and coincidences of the alliance. It is not a static, non-productive period of self-satisfaction but, rather, a highly-rewarding time of collaboration based on recognizing the value of both conscious and unconscious experiences. More relaxed, perhaps, than recent seasons, it is nonetheless a time of fulfilling work, restorative rest and inspiring play.

This hexagram is paired with its complement, 22, IDEAL.

Hexagram Sequence

After things have gained equal footing, they forego contending:
Contentment is the face of ecstasy.

When *Divine Light* and *Divine Shadow* are harmoniously balanced, the lived life within the world of manifestation and the soul's experiences within the world of pre-manifestation are so closely-linked that it seems impossible to imagine being happier, more at ease and less troubled in heart and mind. Moments become hours, hours become days, days become months, months become years: time becomes a seamless series of enjoyable events and illuminating states. One's actions express one's intent perfectly, others' actions are messages writ in fire. The unknown is meaningful and the unknowable a revelation. Truth speaks from every leaf and pebble. Sea and sky whisper the first story over and over. Chance events fall like lightning, provoking laughter like thunder. Things follow one another, sometimes forward, sometimes backward. Deep, passionate friendships come and go. Days go by without a single thought rising unbidden. Clouds are the world's dreams, seasons its moods. Where does the timeless begin and time end? A great pyramid is built of small stones, the ecstatic life of small contentments.

Mantic Formula

The soul draws the divine close:
You are cradled in buoyant light.

Where the world of manifestation and the world of pre-manifestation meet, a rainbow bridge. Perhaps. A shimmering, without doubt; difficult to draw into proper focus, the northern lights shifting to and fro. A Way, the White Road, the Cloud Serpent, the bridge of stars. Perhaps. A vastness, lightning-filled and thunder-struck, a wild chaos in florid bloom, no guardians at the gate save the few gargoyles holding up the rearguard of the last Age. A place of strange images morphing into one another along a drifting boundary between waking and dreaming. A place of madness for the uninitiated. A place of untroubled transition for the initiated, the well-worn path Home. As a whole, this formula signifies that you are attuned to the mystical marriage of the Creative Forces, the Source of symbols coming and going between the World Body and the World Soul.

INTENT

Bottom Line. Well being: The spirit of nature dwelling in purest joy.

Second Line. Well being: Civilization consecrated to the lifelong joy of each individual.

Third Line. Well being: Every individual acting according to their angelic nature.

Fourth Line. Well being: The World Soul providing safe refuge for all souls.

Fifth Line. Well being: Governments cured of competition, fear and domination.

Top Line. Well being: Religions cured of hatred, arrogance and zealotry.

42

IRRATIONALITY

OUTER NATURE: **FIRE**
INNER NATURE: **WATER**

Water within, Fire without: Mystery within, Knowledge without

Fire outside symbolizes acquired knowledge, while Water inside symbolizes one's own mysterious nature. Fire on water: the height of absurdity. Absurdity as the highest form of metaphysics. To grapple with understanding the material world of manifestation without a firm footing in the incongruity of existence is to lose one's balance and fall prey to illusion and manipulation. One's own mysterious nature confronts the acquired knowledge one has gleaned from the conventional wisdom prevalent in one's lifetime—it is extremely difficult to describe the effect of such social conditioning on people because the depths to which it informs their worldview, both of their environment and themselves, is so ingrained as to make it nearly impossible to change. It is, in fact, the very height of absurdity. Even a cursory glance at human civilization demonstrates the utter irrationality upon which it is based—that it continues to desecrate nature and human nature, fully aware of the self-destruction to which it leads, demonstrates the power of social conditioning to elicit behavior in direct opposition to survival. On the whole, it can simply be labeled, *unconscionable*, and set aside as unworthy of further consideration—the initiated constantly face the dilemma of whether it is essentially futile to try to counterbalance the direction and momentum of social indoctrination. Even at relatively close quarters, in teacher-student relationships, the degree to which the student holds to an ego-identity formed by social and historical forces often proves too great for the student to overcome and recover their true self. It is imperative that the contentment of the initiated not lull them into over-generalizing wellbeing and ignoring the mental and emotional anguish that the uninitiated endure for lack of a meaningful alternative to their artificial lifeway. There is little more irrational than living an irrational life, knowing it is utterly irrational.

This hexagram is paired with its complement, 21, RATIONALITY.

HEXAGRAM SEQUENCE

After things have achieved peace of mind, they encounter the miraculous:
IRRATIONALITY is the impossible source of the possible.

The greater part of the absurdity of the world of manifestation is how radically different the metaphysical entity, *absurdity*, displays itself in the pre-manifestation realm of the World Soul. By *metaphysical entity*, is meant, *transcendental entity*—an entity, because it is a symbol-being in the *Pure Idea* realm, and transcendental, because it can be experienced by the soul but not comprehended by human intellect. Its reverse nature in the manifestation and pre-manifestation realms is indicative of its utterly irrational character.

Tranquility of heart-mind opens the soul to extended moments of transcendent clarity of perception. This state of being is free of rational thought, having returned to its original state of essence, a *being-with* the *psychic substance* of the primordial imagination. Within the World Soul, the soul knows only those boundaries it imposes on itself. As it comes to trust the Universal Intent of the Imaginal, the soul becomes more and more identified with the flux of the *psychic substance*, eventually extending its perceptions to the boundaries of the realm of the World Soul itself—this carries it to the juncture of the next higher emanation, that of the realm of Pure Mind. The frontier between the realms of World Soul and Pure Mind is vastly different than that between those of the World Soul and World Body: here, a threshold extends palpably as a sphere touching a sphere, a window open onto the world of giants. Giants, they are called because of their enormity: archangels they are called, as well, because of their purity. The symbol-beings one glimpses—or encounters, upon passing within—are not of shifting *psychic substance* but eternal *Pure Idea*. Here, the *living thoughts* of the *One* take their being beyond all rational reason because they are all born of the same instant in the primordial Act of Creation and bound together by higher-order reason—*spiritual intuition*—which is a net of simultaneity, the orderedness of which, the *law of spiritual cause-*

and-effect, appears altogether acausal to rational logic. The soul entering this realm is not unlike the child walking through a forest of redwood trees: great diamond-beings of infinite perfections form a forest of ever-skyward-reaching monuments—*diamond-beings* because even though eternal and perfect, each affords an infinite number of facets into its symbol-being, so that its meanings are, ultimately, uncountable. Souls that stay in this realm long enough cannot help but feel they are experiencing the One Mind as directly as possible while maintaining a sense of personal awareness.

It is true that the path of return to the *One* runs through this realm—but it is likewise true that the soul may ascend, following the trail of irrationality, into this realm in order to return back to the World Soul, like Prometheus with fire, with the miracle of *enantiodromia*, the supernatural ability to awaken souls to their own opposite.

Mantic Formula

The soul throws one outward:
You leap into the Ulterior and make it your home.

There is nothing more irrational than death in light of the immortality of all things. One's body is the emanation of one's soul within the manifestation realm. One's soul is the emanation of one's pure idea within the pre-manifestation realm. At the birth of its body, the higher soul takes a spark of the *divine fire* from its corresponding pure idea and implants it in the newborn; as the person grows with exposure to the world of manifestation, a lower soul is likewise born and grows. The *divine spark* acts like a homing beacon in the natural course of events, drawing the lower soul ever closer to the fated reunion with the higher soul. This reunion benefits both souls at the death of the body, since they can return Home together. However, many people do not follow the natural course of events and their lower soul neither longs for nor finds their higher soul during their lifetime. In such cases, the higher soul of Understanding returns Home without the memory of the mortal lifetime, while the lower soul of Memory wanders lost, without any understanding of its situation, *in the borderland* between the pre-manifestation and the manifestation realms. Without understanding of its predicament and with only memories of its lifetime, it settles into a routine of reliving those memories over and over, imagining it's still alive in body. Part of the ancients' wisdom teachings reveal that one's mere presence among such disoriented lower souls acts as a catalyst, like a surrogate higher soul's understanding, to rouse them from their stupor and spur them on to reunite with their higher soul immediately. This is sacred work, to be undertaken only by those souls who have completely divested themselves of self-centeredness and self-importance. As a whole, this formula signifies that you do not hesitate to venture out into the *intermediate realm* in order to awaken the dead to their immortality.

INTENT

Bottom Line. Divine delirium: Tears of the gods bathe nature in bees and butterflies.

Second Line. Divine delirium: Ghosts of the living run on ahead.

Third Line. Divine delirium: Living time pours from the navel of the sky.

Fourth Line. Divine delirium: The stone arrow returns from the spirit world.

Fifth Line. Divine delirium: Peace is the baptism of fire for the shadow-souled.

Top Line. Divine delirium: Cradled in fire, runes of the origin augur wondrous impossibilities.

43

REFINING

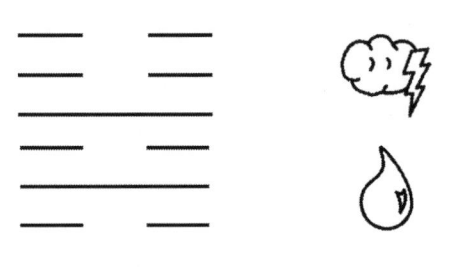

OUTER NATURE: LIGHTNING
INNER NATURE: WATER

Water within, Lightning without: Mystery within, Motivation without

Lightning outside symbolizes incitement, while Water inside symbolizes one's own mysterious nature. Within the physical endowment of a body, there are few things more mysterious to the conscious mind than the instincts. The initiated do not attempt to understand the instincts but, rather, to convert their substantial energy into constructive works that benefit others. This is accomplished, first and foremost, by recognizing the symbolic meaning of each instinct, reading that symbol as deeply as possible in order to embody the full range of its meanings and then continue to observe it in order to track any changes in either behavior or meaning. Eating, for example, is such a symbol. Abiding with it, soaking it in, penetrating its outer cover of behavior, searching for its divine message as an emanation of the World Soul, the initiated find an entry point when viewing *eating* as *the most frequent conscious activity physically connecting the body to the world*. In other words, on a symbolic level, human nature is eating the world, since *food* can readily be interpreted as *physically nourishing part of the world*. A particularly powerful symbol—on a universal level—that meshes human life in daily rituals of eating parts of the World Body. Just this superficial of a reading can alter the meaning of an instinct and then the behavior itself of the consciously embodied instinct; the meaning, in other words may alter the attitude of the behavior, *refining* it within the pre-manifestation realm, which then emanates into the manifestation realm. Initiates may, of course, delve deeper into such a symbol, tracing their *subjective* meanings, as well—an activity that often ensures an even more profound refinement of attitude and enactment of the instinct.

This hexagram is paired with its complement, 20, TRADITION.

Hexagram Sequence

After things have plumbed the shadows, they draw them back into the light:
Refining is spiritualizing the instincts.

The blacksmith heats the metal, pounds the metal into shape, cools the metal, repeats the cycle many times over: *tempering*. The alternation of heating and cooling the metal changes its nature, making it both stronger and more resilient. A similar process is at work in the sequence of hexagrams, which alternates between opposing-complementary states in order to increase both the strength and reliance of the soul—an effect that emanates into the lower soul within the world of manifestation.

The instincts are the base elements of the lower soul. This is not to denigrate or desecrate them, which social institutions often do even as they take advantage of them to indoctrinate human nature. Viewing the base elements from the perspective of alchemy honors them, acknowledging them as the foundation from which the subtle, or refined, substance is composed. It is axiomatic in alchemy that if one wishes to produce gold from the base elements, then one must recognize that the base already possesses, no matter how small a quantity, a particulate of gold essence within it. All of alchemy is, of course, a science of transforming the lower nature of individuals into the higher nature—the transmutation of the instincts and their emotions into the angelic nature of the higher soul. This transmutation is only possible if the instincts are honored as already possessing a part of the nature of angelic beings—and this is certainly the case, although not always recognized by individuals, as the higher soul informs the lower soul at the birth of the body with a spark of the *divine fire* of the *One*.

Mantic Formula

Everything spawns:
You return to the source of the homing instinct.

The emotions of the instincts are the passions and desires of aversion and attachment. They constitute a large part of the conscious experience of the instincts. Fear and hatred are examples of passions of aversion, while lust and envy are examples of passions of attachment. Obviously, these are part of the base elements to be transmuted into more sublime manifestations. At the lowest point in a person's experience, however, these form constellations of fused passions that blind the mind and cloud the heart. Such *darkenings* of the soul announce a *turning point* in a person's spiritual advance. By investigating these passions from the inside, it is possible for one to convert them into symbols—both universal and personal—that reflect their original divine nature: this reflection reorients one to the true lifeway, transforming the mortal passions into the angelic longings. The way back to the *One* is through the *Many*. As a whole, this formula signifies that you follow the conch's song of homesickness back to the homebound sea.

INTENT

Bottom Line. Universal threshold: The distillation of human nature liberating nature.

Second Line. Universal threshold: The Dreamer of the Great Dream awakens within the Dream.

Third Line. Universal threshold: The blacksmith forges the shaman in the furnace of the World Egg.

Fourth Line. Universal threshold: The Book of Destiny is writ in reverse.

Fifth Line. Universal threshold: Watchtowers and ramparts lie in ruins for lack of need.

Top Line. Universal threshold: A unicorn resting beside the oasis of absolute purity.

44

IMPROVISATION

OUTER NATURE: **WIND**
INNER NATURE: **WATER**

Water within, Wind without: Mystery within, Adaptation without

Wind outside symbolizes adapting to circumstances, while Water inside symbolizes one's own mysterious nature. The initiated view life within the world of manifestation as a Sacred Game—they cannot anticipate how their own unknown potential might respond to circumstances as they arise, but they *can* sense the intrinsic significance every moment carries into the eternal significance coursing through All Creation. Which is to say, every act—internal or external—is a tributary of meaning flowing into the great river of meaning embodied in the *first and last symbol* that is All Creation. In the act of *sacred play*, the initiated are both player *and* piece: the body and its lower soul are a piece being moved within the Sacred Game, while the higher soul is making the corresponding moves within the pre-manifestation realm. It is a *Game* because it has rules that bind it in cohesion: the law of spiritual cause-and-effect. It is *Sacred* because it makes the divine language flesh: in its inner workings and mysterious relationships, it is the holiest symbol of itself, the *open secret* of the interplay of fate and freedom.

This hexagram is paired with its complement, 19, RELEARNING.

Hexagram Sequence

After things have been purified, they revert to innocence:
IMPROVISATION is unpremeditated being.

One need not ever write a word of poetry to live a poetic life. What passes through the poetic heart is rid of routinized thought and trivialized imagination, both characteristics of those who have fallen lockstep onto the path of fate. The poetic heart is a symbol of the Poetic Imagination, which is the living expression of the individual's direct experience of the *Imaginal*, the primordial and fundamental imagination at the core of the soul. The essence of all things is *eternal change*, which itself is the result of *eternal renewal*. Creation is a wellspring of renewal, bubbling up before one's eyes everywhere. The relationships between things and their interchanges of energy is complex and highly unpredictable, a direct manifestation of the Great Mystery. *As Above, So Below*: one's own mysterious nature is a microcosm of the macrocosm of the Great Mystery, establishing one's capacity to adapt readily and spontaneously to the ever-changing renewal of Creation. Adaptation to the Great Mystery is not, for the initiated, the final aim—they seek to express their unique relationship with Creation in a likewise unique way: the poetic life follows the path of *freedom* and expresses itself in moments of *beauty*. *Freedom*, in this sense, means *unpremeditated actions*—either internal or external—that lead to the fullest appreciation of All Creation and, thereby, to the ecstatic life. *Beauty*, in this sense, means *uncontrived interpretation* of the divine meaning within each thing and, therefore, every experience. Improvisation, then, is freedom from forethought and ulterior motive in one's extemporaneous embodiment of the poetic life.

Mantic Formula

The soul does not in stagnation dwell:
You keep moving.

The omnipresent and continuous renewal of Creation is exemplified by the concurrent flow of Wind and Water: unceasing, ever-changing, dancing, soaring, delving, colliding, disappearing, reappearing—profound mysterious action redoubled within infinite adaptations. The way wind and water move across the landscape is a direct manifestation of the way that intent moves through *psychic substance*—it follows the lines of collective usage, pooling in places of high tradition, roaring round summits of individual vision, cascading through ancient dark motives, hovering amid vast arrays of flowering peace. For the initiated, even holding still and concentrating is continuing to move. Everything is practice for something else—all is unforeseeable, even the depths of the present moment, so all is the honing of skills and perceptions in the continuing practice of improvisation. As a whole, this formula signifies that you move moment-by-moment, co-creating with Creation, in the Sacred Game of making the divine language flesh.

INTENT

Bottom Line. Unforeseen yoking: Spirit and land unite in Dreamtime.

Second Line. Unforeseen sameness: Spirit and land unite in Dreamtime.

Third Line. Unforeseen adapting: Spirit and land unite in Dreamtime.

Fourth Line. Unforeseen contraction: Spirit and land unite in Dreamtime.

Fifth Line. Unforeseen ritual: Spirit and land unite in Dreamtime.

Top Line. Unforeseen secret: Spirit and land unite in Dreamtime.

45

UNCERTAINTY

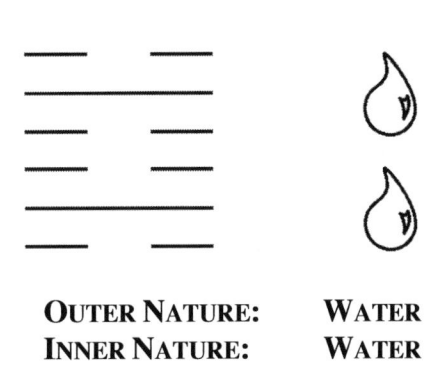

OUTER NATURE:	WATER
INNER NATURE:	WATER

Water within, Water without: Mystery within, Mystery without

Water outside symbolizes the Great Mystery of All Creation, while Water inside symbolizes one's own mysterious nature forever hidden from full conscious knowledge. The Great Mystery is the unfathomable and inexplicable *reality* of All, while one's own mysterious nature is the unfathomable and inexplicable *reality* of the individual. The expression *reality* is one seldom used by the initiated because actual reality, as opposed to conceptions of reality, is, by experience, unfathomable and inexplicable. Beyond the grasp of intelligence either in experience or contemplation, *reality* is the Great Mystery of existence. When the sages of old were asked about the truth of reality, their reply was universally the same: *I do not know*. To speak of the Primordial Uncertainty with any pretense of certainty has always been tantamount to espousing bad teachings and courting bad luck.

Nonetheless, what *is* known about the Unknowable? Just this—that without the Unknown, All would fall into the Known and constitute the fixed path of predictable, predestined, unalterable fate. Corollary to that axiom is this—without the Unknown, no well of potential would exist from which Creation might draw in its continuing act of surging forth the new, original, ever-changing, unpredictable *sacred play* of freedom. In this sense, *reality* appears to hold more in common with a Sacred Game of Chance than with a materialistic cause-and-effect mechanism in the process of winding down. To speak like this of the Primordial Uncertainty is to articulate some of its more obvious effects, much as nothing can be known about the inside of a black hole for certain, despite conclusions drawn from its effects on its surroundings; it is not to attempt to speak directly about the Great Mystery Itself.

This hexagram is paired with its complement, 18, CERTAINTY.

HEXAGRAM SEQUENCE

After things have attained spontaneity, they are embraced by chance:
UNCERTAINTY is living potential.

The continued unfolding of Creation advances according to the law of spiritual of cause-and-effect, moving through the spontaneity of Improvisation, into the Uncertainty of chance. This movement through poetic freedom, into the mystic's immersion in the Great Mystery, marks the forward thrust of awareness as it transmutes the art of interpretation into the *state of innocence*, thereby returning the soul to its primordial condition of the *inner void*. This reversion is one of having no representations of, or associations to, any concepts or interpretations of experience. *All* is unknown: awareness encounters but does not recognize. *All* is unknowable: the scale, depth and intensity of raw experience transcends the *original innocence* of awareness as it first emanates from the *One* and encounters the overwhelming grandeur of Creation. The rational intelligence, no matter how advanced, is unable to escape being a living part of the *Living Whole* it encounters: *reality* is alive and aware—the *One*, the *Absolute*, the *Monad*, the *Tao*. It is a *Living Reality*, ever-changing and ever-renewing, a *living potential* without end, limit or impossibility.

In the scale of eternity, from Creation to Completion, *Living Reality* manifests as a constantly shape-shifting entity with no knowable characteristics. But that is on a scale of time impossible to accurately envision. On the scale of geological time, or even astronomical time, however, *Living Reality* manifests as the Pattern of Order and Chance. *Order* signifies those structures that persist relatively unchanged over long periods of time, structures that provide the framework, the *rules*, so to speak, of the Sacred Game. *Chance*, in this sense, signifies the *sacred play* within the framework, each utterly new, utterly distinct, utterly unpredictable move of the game or throw of the dice. The ancients called this pattern, *mountains and rivers*, where the image is of ever-changing flowing rivers running between solid mountains—

mountains symbolizing the *order* of the unchanging, and *rivers* symbolizing the *chance* flux of change. One may learn the rules of a game of dice but that has very little indeed to do with the lived experience of casting caution to the wind and gambling everything on a single throw of the dice.

MANTIC FORMULA

The Great Mystery comes forth like a cataract vaulting into an abyss:
You plunge into the Deep like the spirit of water itself.

There were alliances of ancient savants who called themselves, *Idiots*, who practiced a form of wisdom called, *Mindlessness*—a practice of *inner fasting*, of leaning into each moment with no preconceptions, no opinions, no ideas about what to expect, no ideas about how to respond to what they might encounter. The wisest of the wise, when encountering the Grand Uncertainty of existence, rather than blinking and backing away, engaged the Great Mystery with a sense of celebration and exploration. Every moment new, every moment different, every moment without precedent—little different than making one's way through an uncharted rain forest of impenetrable vines: every step new, every step different, every step without precedent. Spiritual authenticity requires an utterly open heart-mind, unconditioned by past experience. No matter how concrete an experience and certain an interpretation one might have, that does not mean that *reality*, the *living being*, is not metamorphosing further. Within the pre-manifestation realm of the World Soul, this phase of spiritual cause-and-effect is sometimes likened to an earthquake—or to a wet dog shaking off water: all of *psychic substance* is temporarily shaken free, uprooted, from a sense of permanence and disarrayed in a welter of coincidence, where it might transform into *anything*. It is, therefore, a phase within which concentrated purity of intent is absolutely necessary in order to: prevent malintended souls from interrupting one's alliance's beneficial endeavors; take advantage of the natural disruption in malintended endeavors by nurturing their latent beneficial natures; and, take advantage of the unsettled nature of *psychic substance* to create new, previously unimaginable, endeavors. In this way, misfortune in the manifestation realm may be avoided and good fortune evoked. As a whole, this formula signifies that you throw yourself into the center of the world and emerge from the other side.

INTENT

Bottom Line. Silent dark: Great-souled beings performing acts of anonymous benevolence.

Second Line. Silent dark: The night fuses all distinctions into a single world.

Third Line. Silent dark: The celestial landscape is within.

Fourth Line. Silent dark: It is the sounds that cannot be heard that produce total harmony.

Fifth Line. Silent dark: Aligning with the immortal game of chance, not the mortal rule of order.

Top Line. Silent dark: The ancient gods and goddesses are the first psychic substance.

46

PRACTICE

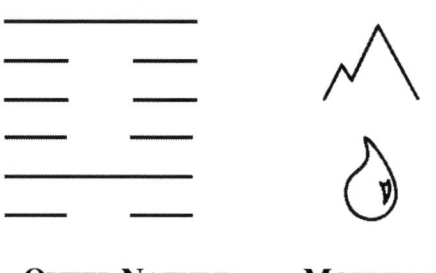

OUTER NATURE: MOUNTAIN
INNER NATURE: WATER

Water within, Mountain without: Mystery within, Incubation without

Mountain outside symbolizes calm, while Water inside symbolizes one's own mysterious nature. The sages of old handed down time-tested techniques of actualizing the *innate perfectibility* of human nature, the result of which is the attainment of the *ecstatic life,* coincident with an *awakened heart-mind*. From their own experience, the ancients knew that actualizing this potential would resolve the long-term problems facing life in the manifestation realm—nearly all of which stem from the desecration of nature and human nature. The image is of a Mountain of stillness perfecting the Water of one's own mysterious nature. For the uninitiated, stillness is difficult to marshal because of the flood of habit thoughts, emotions and memories pouring forth from their own mysterious nature—rather than stillness exerting a positive effect on their mysterious nature, their mysterious nature exerts a disruptive effect on stillness. For the initiated, however, this phase of the practice is a continuation of the self-discipline they consistently apply to quieting the *habit heart-mind without* quieting the *ecstatic heart-mind*: here, the self-defeating habits of their own mysterious nature are permanently stilled, while the self-creating spontaneous aspects rejoice in reverence and awe.

This hexagram is paired with its complement, 17, BELONGING.

Hexagram Sequence

After things have wed coincidence, they act without striving:
Practice is purposeful purposelessness.

Those who help weave the web of living coincidences find they have crossed the threshold of inner peace: they find themselves so attuned to the mysterious manner in which things fall together that they recognize the futility of striving for objectives. It is as if one leapt into a wild river and then spent all one's efforts trying to swim upstream—of course one would recognize the folly of such striving. Letting go of the need to struggle takes great courage and trust in life. Allowing the current of the river to take one where it will at the pace it will—this is not the lifeway of the conditioned human nature, which has been indoctrinated to suspect threats to its security everywhere. Striving to control events only makes matter worse, but that does not stop people from trying. Responding to events without any sense of purpose in mind, the initiated allow the flux of the river to carry them along where it will at the pace it will. To be in harmonious balance with the Whole—this is the practice of the immortals. Stilling the body's habit thoughts, emotions, memories and sensations while rousing the heart-mind to recognize its own mysterious nature—this is the ancients' practice of inner peace.

Mantic Formula

Musicians and athletes train for mastery:
You hone your intent for corresponding mastery.

The path to mastery is not a mysterious one. It simply requires strict training: unbeckoned thoughts are intrusive thoughts, products of the habit mind that falls by routine into passive non-attentive states not too dissimilar to sleepwalking. To keep the mind actively attentive is a matter of intent, which, within the World Soul, is the manner in which one encounters and responds to the other entities and their intentions within the *psychic substance*—it is a state of *active receptivity*, wherein no unbidden thoughts intrude but the soul is keenly sensitive and receptive to the fluctuations in the pre-manifestation realm. Within the manifestation realm, this practice has many offshoots utilizing various methods of self-realization protocols—some direct lineage teachings, but most adaptive conventions accommodating the passivity of the modern mind. The latter practices are called long path, or gradual enlightenment, teachings, whereas the former are known as short path, or sudden enlightenment, teachings. It is the body, after all, that must awaken to the enlightened soul, so all the obstacles to awakening are of the body's own doing and must be removed by the body's own efforts: to release the effortless spontaneous flow of heart-mind into the triple world of nature, humankind and spirit, it is necessary to eradicate every form of inner resistance to nature, humankind and spirit. The short path teachings are straightforward in this regard: still the habit heart-mind while rousing the living heart-mind—this opens awareness to clearly hearing the divine voice speaking within by quieting the compulsive thoughts trying to drown it out. As a whole, this formula signifies that you maintain constant and continual focus of your intent on sustaining the unbroken state of *active receptivity*.

INTENT

Bottom Line. Free thought: Butterflies basking in the meadow's sunlight.

Second Line. Free thought: Ice on a frozen river cracking and breaking up in Springtide.

Third Line. Free thought: A child's imagination roams without care across land, sea and sky.

Fourth Line. Free thought: A raft without anchor of precedent or tiller of reason drifts aimlessly.

Fifth Line. Free thought: The music of the spheres beginning a new symphony.

Top Line. Free thought: Joyously following the ancients' footsteps.

47

ENTRAINING

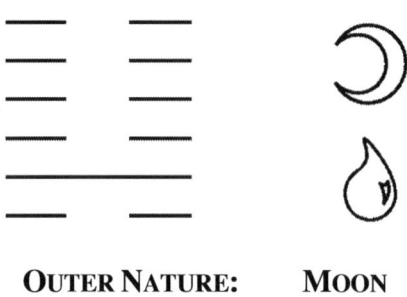

OUTER NATURE:	MOON
INNER NATURE:	WATER

Water within, Moon without: Mystery within, Completion without

Moon outside symbolizes realization of potential, while Water inside symbolizes one's own mysterious nature. Embodying the *spiritual practice* of the ancients leads to the realization of potential—this acts as a catalyst for one's own mysterious nature, drawing it further along the inner path, further into the inner landscape, further within the *Heart of Creation*. The obstacle to *reality* that the uninitiated suffer is a lack of sensitivity to the range of Life in all its possible manifestations, including the *underlying reality* of the *Living Whole*—the constant distraction of compulsive thoughts and obsessive self-interestedness deaden the subtle senses and encapsulate people in an echo chamber of separateness from, and mistrust of, the Whole. The realization of potential means that the seed comes to full fruition, that the promise is fulfilled: the sunflower turns to follow the sun as it courses the day sky, the moonflower synchronizes its blooming with the night—these entrainments are often triggered by natural cues, called *zeitgebers*, or *time givers*, that pull lifeforms along with the rhythms of day and night and the seasons of the year. Within the pre-manifestation world, the soul encounters idiosyncratic image-symbols that act as mnemonic cues to trigger its entrainment to the *living intent* of the *psychic substance* itself. To realize the potential of one's own mysterious nature is to make conscious its *revealing and re-veiling* of the divine symbols—implanted in antique times by the soul-making archangels—in order to discover its spontaneous synchronization to the emergence of divine symbols from the *psychic substance* itself. This phase of Creation's unfolding enfolds the soul in a timeless period of unforeseeable and profoundly meaningful coincidences that vivify the intent and assure further entrainment of those divine image-symbols into the world of manifestation.

This hexagram is paired with its complement, 16, CONCEPTION.

HEXAGRAM SEQUENCE

After things have become rudderless, they are carried by the Current:
ENTRAINING is falling into step with the Way.

To be rudderless is to be purposefully purposeless, to practice the art of *Mindlessness*, to set aside every expectation of, and association with, events external or internal—so doing brings one into alignment with the living *Current of Change* and its intent to explore every possible meaning of every possible symbol of Creation. Beneath the *Current of Change*, of course, lies the *Bedrock of the Unchanging*—it is of these two that the *Universal Tao* is comprised, just as a river requires the current of water flowing over the fixed course of the riverbed. This *Living Course* of change and the unchanging, of the current and the bedrock that are one—this is the *Universal Tao*, and it is with this *Living Course* that one's own *individual tao* of *Mindlessness* aligns. Wide awake, unbroken alertness, vivid presence, tranquil mind, open heart, welcoming spirit, harmonious soul—such are the descriptors of the initiated practitioners of *Mindlessness*.

MANTIC FORMULA

The moon is the mother of the sea:
You ebb and flow with the tides.

The higher soul continually makes welcome an alignment with the lower soul, that the work in the manifest realm and the pre-manifest realm might constitute a single intent; but the vast majority of people live their lives in the manifestation realm without ever recognizing the existence of either the higher soul or the World Soul. Many of the savants of old called that tragic state one of *sleepwalking*, for such individuals believe themselves awake and oriented, yet they are trapped in a world cut off from their higher functioning. Unconscious of their true condition, they stumble in the dark from one perilous situation to another.

The *Heartbeat of Creation* is palpable to those sensitized to their own mysterious nature: the inner path passes through their *living mystery* and enters the *Living Sphere of Reality* in a single step: it is like musicians playing a song—they all adhere to the same rhythm, the same timing, which carries them along in a state of communion. Yet the *rhythm* is not any individual's; nor is it even any song's. It is a universal element of the *Living Whole*, an echo of the *Heartbeat of Creation* to which individuals attune themselves and thereby move with all the grace, beauty and power rightfully attributed to authentic co-creators of *living reality*. The moon gives birth to the tides; the tides give birth to one's own mysterious rhythm. One therefore follows one's own rhythm back through the tides and the phases of the moon to return to the very first *Heartbeat of Creation*, in order to begin again, with the *Grand Alliance* at the primordial Act of Creation. As a whole, this formula signifies that you move through this lifetime with practiced ease and grace, a vital part of the *Living Whole* that wants the best for you and all others at the same time.

INTENT

Bottom Line. Angelic timing: A rainstorm of Autumn leaves.

Second Line. Angelic timing: The inevitable flowering of the Golden Age of Humanity.

Third Line. Angelic timing: Awakening arriving in this lifetime.

Fourth Line. Angelic timing: The homunculus departs the retort on midnight of the winter solstice.

Fifth Line. Angelic timing: Living secrets withdrawing further back into the shrouding mists.

Top Line. Angelic timing: Ritual opens the gate for the mystic to enter.

48

EMBODYING

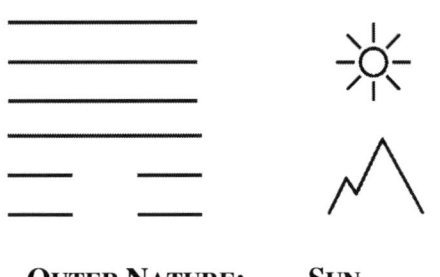

OUTER NATURE:	SUN
INNER NATURE:	MOUNTAIN

Mountain within, Sun without: Incubation within, Creation without

Sun outside symbolizes origin, while Mountain inside symbolizes incubation. One of the great mysteries of All Creation is how entities from one state of density come to embodiment in another state of density. This is as miraculous in their descent through forms of emanations as it is in their return ascent. The *One* embodies within *Pure Idea*, which embodies within *Soul*, which embodies within *Manifestation*; even more telling is the progressive etherealization of each embodiment in its return from *Manifestation* to *Soul* to *Pure Idea* to the *One*.

Mountain symbolizes stillness and tranquility, calm and stability, stopping and holding; it is the chrysalis and the egg, within which the seed of life is protected and nurtured until it is prepared for Life—and it is the prayer or meditation state in which the seed of spirit is protected and nurtured until it is prepared for the Spirit World. This seed of life or seed of spirit is Sun, which symbolizes creation and origin, seed and potential, birth and beginning. As great a mystery as *Embodying* is, it reveals its fundamental equation in its relationship between Mountain and Sun: the living seed of potential is protected and nurtured within the stillness and tranquility of the initiated heart-mind.

This hexagram is paired with its complement, 15, SHEDDING.

HEXAGRAM SEQUENCE

After things have realized at-one-ment, they become ritual itself:
EMBODYING is immovable wisdom.

Establishing stillness and tranquility of heart-mind identifies *Embodying* as a continuation of the *Mindlessness* praxis. Removing oneself from the center of one's own attention allows awareness to experience *reality-as-it-is* by quieting the habit mind and activating unconditional receptivity via original mind. Original mind is here cocooned in tranquil stillness, wherein it can also cultivate the continuation of *Entraining* to the Highest Good. In this way, one moves from one's current embodiment into the next: the seed is sown in the ground of peace.

The initiated become a *living ritual*, whose every thought, word and act consecrates the Eternal Moment, imaged as the *sacred mountain* of immovable wisdom. Embodying *living wisdom* is the *living ritual* of the initiated: their wisdom, though alive, is *immovable* because it remains constant throughout every incarnation within every emanation. Their wisdom, moreover, is *alive*, not just in the sense of living within the heart-mind of an embodied being, but *alive forever* in the sense of the continuous lineage of wisdom teachings surviving from the sages of the previous Age and guiding the founding of the coming Age.

MANTIC FORMULA

Radiant awareness fills the cloudless sky:
You fill the carefree body as well.

Living wisdom is embodied in the ritual of moment-to-moment existence in the sense that it must be applied to experience in a way consistent *both* with the wisdom teachings *and* the realities of the historical era in which one finds oneself. This is what makes it *living ritual*—it is not static form holding on to old dogma, but the living adaptation of time-proven wisdom to the experiential concerns of embodied beings. It runs counter to all forms of static ritual based on the re-enactment of domination by some beings of their peers or their environment. *Living wisdom*, in other words, cannot be separate from *Universal Love* and its care for all beings at the same time. Static forms masquerading as practical wisdom that justifies all manner of domination through sophisticated rationalizations has as much to do with *living wisdom* as a fireplace to a mermaid. Embodying the living wisdom of *Mindlessness* is like conscious light filling the cloudless sky—of course the untroubled spirit is embodied just so! As a whole, this formula signifies that you embody the freedom of spirit to ascend and descend at will among the emanations.

INTENT

Bottom Line. Seed ferry: The most fragile idea in the world is nature.

Second Line. Seed ferry: The most fragile idea in nature is humaneness.

Third Line. Seed ferry: The most fragile idea in humaneness is evolution.

Fourth Line. Seed ferry: The most fragile idea in evolution is freedom.

Fifth Line. Seed ferry: The most fragile idea in freedom is history.

Top Line. Seed ferry: The most fragile idea in history is solidarity.

49

COMMUNION

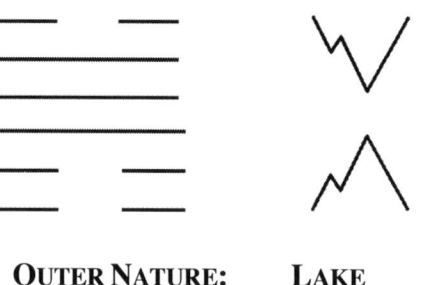

OUTER NATURE:	LAKE
INNER NATURE:	MOUNTAIN

Mountain within, Lake without: Incubation within, Wonder without

Lake outside symbolizes wonder and awe, while Mountain inside symbolizes contemplative stillness. True, living, wisdom does not throw the soul into a foreign and unwelcoming land, only to make an exile of it. On the contrary, *living wisdom* is the therapeutic to that feeling of banishment resulting from misinterpretations of the nature of self and Creation. Misinterpreting the nature of self, the uninitiated *mistake a thief for their son*, which is the ancients' way of saying that people mistake the habit mind for their true self. Misinterpreting the nature of Creation, the uninitiated suspect its vastness and inhuman nature as a complete disregard for human nature; from such a perspective, individuals are born for no reason other than—at best—of playing out a particular alternative pathway in nature's genetic code. At worst, there is no reason for human existence nor is there any meaning to it—people are merely an accident of nature and their consciousness even more so an accident and even less so meaningful. So distasteful to most people's thoughts are these that they carry them around unconsciously, rationalizing and constantly commenting on experience to keep them at a distance. As a symptom of their generalized distrust of Creation, however, these suspicions, no matter how unconscious, profoundly affect the worldview of the modern mind. As the ancients taught: *You cannot be exiled, for you have not ever, in truth, left home.*

This hexagram is paired with its complement, 14, STEEPING.

Hexagram Sequence

After things have embodied reverence, they reunite with All:
Communion is the Immediacy and Intimacy of selfsameness.

The path of true, living, wisdom transforms the sage into the mystic. Wisdom is essential to living in harmony with all other beings—knowing the appropriate responses to circumstances, performed at the appropriate time, executed in the appropriate way, with the appropriate intent, for the appropriate reason, all without conscious forethought or consideration: wisdom is key to guiding human nature to a lifeway of balance and harmony. But the *why* of living such a balanced and harmonious lifeway is established not by wisdom, but by the mystical. Wisdom is the shadow of the mystical. Wisdom renders the soul's direct experience of *mystical communion* into spiritually ethical action, both externally and internally. *Living wisdom* is what the initiated reveal, *mystical communion* is what the initiated re-veil. The tranquil stability of Mountain provides the foundation for Lake to respond to the vast, inhuman, universe with wonder, awe, curiosity—and joyous communion with the spirit revealing and re-veiling itself within every embodied being. Recognizing this universal state of selfsameness within All, the soul undergoes that most esoteric of transformations: the *mystical reunion*. Shattering every bond holding the soul, bursting the bubble surrounding the soul, in a moment, an eyeblink, all rushes out as all rushes in—the river rushing to meet the sea as the sea rushes to meet the river. *Reunion of Souls*: the all-at-once return of all souls *Home*. At every turn, recognition of suddenly remembered allies—how could any of them ever be forgotten? Nowhere among the countless souls an unfamiliar, nowhere a soul with whom one does not share an Ages-long history. *Home*—the mystical reunion of immediately being recognized by all and instantly recalling the history shared by all, a single memory of shared history, of universal communion of All awake and aware within the One Mind.

Mantic Formula

The bottomless lake reflects the heavens:
You drift among the constellations.

The *One* has long been experienced by mystics as a great sphere of light from which all its emanations pour forth in its overflowing creative production. *Light*, of course, does not mean the light perceptible to the eye, but rather *conscious light*, the light of radiant awareness, perceptible in its realm to the soul. It *is*, however, this *living light* that emanates as perceptible light within the world of manifestation. The *Sphere of Universal Communion* it has been called, and *Universal Home*, and *Creation*, as well. It is experienced as the origin and destination of all souls and as their eternal dwelling place, as well. *As Above, So Below*: the *One* is a sphere of *aware light*, and every soul, too, as the microcosm of the *One's* macrocosm, is a sphere of *aware light*. The *Sphere of Universal Communion* is All Creation beyond any emanation; it expands and contracts, as if breathing life into the emanations; and at its center the *Home* to which All return and All are sent forth into the tides again. When souls of *aware light* encounter one another and they approach close enough for their surfaces to touch, then in that moment, they achieve *spiritual communion*: instantly, spontaneously, without any conscious intention, the whole of the *Understanding and Memory* of each passes into the other. This *spiritual communion*, though not always conscious, has its correlative manifestation in the *direct transmission* between souls in the realms of the World Soul and the World Body. The expansion and contraction of the *Sphere of Universal Communion* periodically contracts to its least diameter, at which point all souls are drawn together so closely that the surface of each is touched on all sides by the surface of others, so that at that moment all souls are united in a single *spiritual communion* of shared *Understanding and Memory*. The higher soul, though it implants a spark of the divine fire within the lower soul, does not, in truth, ever leave its dwelling place within the *Sphere of Universal Communion*. As a whole, this formula signifies that you answer the call to mystical communion, deepening your experience of the *ecstatic life*.

INTENT

Bottom Line. Shared exchange: A wolf cub growing within the intimacy of the pack.

Second Line. Shared exchange: Common rituals binding the community across time.

Third Line. Shared exchange: Individual rituals binding higher and lower souls across eternity.

Fourth Line. Shared exchange: The mere proximity of a great-souled being breaks the trance.

Fifth Line. Shared exchange: Focused attention on Universal Love breaks open the heart.

Top Line. Shared exchange: Two spheres of aware light touching.

50

RECOLLECTION

OUTER NATURE:	FIRE
INNER NATURE:	MOUNTAIN

Mountain within, Fire without: Incubation within, Knowledge without

Fire outside symbolizes memory, while Mountain inside symbolizes contemplative stillness. *Forgetting* is fundamental and necessary to existence. Without it, awareness would be overwhelmed by the *active memory* of every bit of detail of every experience ever lived, making focusing on the present moment with full concentration all but impossible. Yet, this faculty of forgetting does not mean that experience is actually lost forever—on the contrary, it is relegated to *inactive memory*, where it can be recalled when needed. The nature of the relationship between the individual mind and the One Mind means, however, that there exists a single *active memory* and a single *inactive memory* shared by all beings. Key to gaining entry to this *universal memory* is the practice of *active forgetting*—the technique of cultivating a tranquil and unshakeable individual mind that empties itself of personal thought by consciously relegating all its *active memory* to *inactive memory*. Spirit, like nature, abhors a vacuum: the emptiness created by *active forgetting* calls forth the guardian spirit of the *universal memory*, who allows passage into the *Chamber of Recollection*. Within this depository of all experience, there is no secret of eternity that cannot be recovered: all true learning is an act of recollection.

This hexagram is paired with its complement, 13, SERVICE.

HEXAGRAM SEQUENCE

After things have merged souls, they share memories:
RECOLLECTION is the golden thread of the immortal tapestry.

The communion of all souls establishes the *rite of recollection*, ensuring that no timebound experience is ever lost to eternity. In the vastness of time, all things immortal may become mortal and all things mortal may become immortal—but in the single moment of eternity, all things are immortal. Souls in the pre-manifestation realm of the World Soul manifest within the world of manifestation—they seldom do so alone, however, forming *soul pacts* of mutual benefit with allies who agree to enter the manifestation realm and meet one another at various points in each other's life in order to further their shared purpose. Although individuals may possess some faint intimation of help-to-come, they do not consciously recall their *soul pacts* until actually meeting their ally within the manifestation realm—and even then, it may take repeated contact to break through the social barriers of polite distrust. Even though some such soul pacts result in long, collaborative, relationships, many are sudden, short-lived, unexpected encounters that trigger an inrush of recollections of a magical, nearly miraculous, nature.

MANTIC FORMULA

Time fuses moments into a single space:
You move to and fro at will.

Not every soul harbors the mystic's wish to dissolve back into the *One* at death. Instead, they spend as much time as possible within the World Soul, constructing a dwelling place for themselves and allies: with their intent, they *carve out space* to fashion a home in the pre-manifestation realm in which to dwell between incarnations in the manifestation realm.

There is likewise a secret tradition maintained by indigenous peoples over the millennia that has proven advantageous in face of the encroachment of the modern lifeway upon the ancient. Using their intent within the pre-manifestation realm of the *spirit world* of the World Soul, spiritual leaders guide the community into constructing a homeland there—not one just for their souls upon death, but one in which their souls may dwell, free and autonomous, while their bodies yet reside in the world of manifestation. Such homelands are embodiments of intentional memory, fortresses of *psychic substance* so concentrated by righteous valor, undefeatable spirit and strategic mockery that they resist the siege of materialism.

As a whole, this formula signifies that you recognize that time—*living time*—is the embodiment of *living memory* that holds all beings within its *Chamber of Recollection*.

INTENT

Bottom Line. Iron mountain: A generation of intelligentsia investigating the immaterial half of nature.

Second Line. Iron mountain: A genealogy of all the souls ever dwelling in Creation.

Third Line. Iron mountain: A treasure trove of secret books detailing the ancients' wisdom teachings.

Fourth Line. Iron mountain: An abandoned nest in a withered tree.

Fifth Line. Iron mountain: A spirit medium helping a family receive advice from an ancestor.

Top Line. Iron mountain: A hooded figure with a lantern searching the labyrinth of universal memory.

51

CONCENTRATION

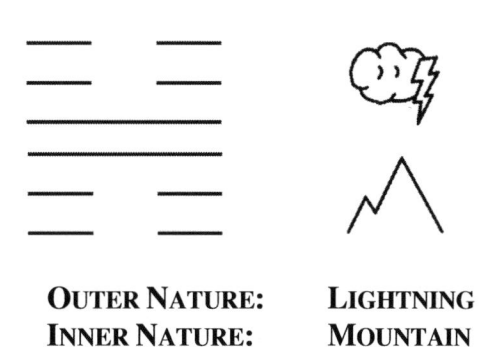

| OUTER NATURE: | LIGHTNING |
| INNER NATURE: | MOUNTAIN |

Mountain within, Lightning without: Incubation within, Motivation without

Lightning outside symbolizes inspiration, while Mountain inside symbolizes stability. Lightning strikes the mountaintop: it is an event that occurs at the highest point of the earth and the lowest point of the sky, the meeting place of form and the formless. It is the domain of *living symbols*, whose images constitute their descent into form and whose meanings constitute their ascent into formlessness. A symbol's image, in other words, makes its form approachable by rational thought but permits nothing more refined than literal interpretation. A symbol's meaning, on the other hand, withdraws ever skyward, ever further into the formlessness of ever more metaphorical and, therefore, transcendent interpretations. The mountain-mind of stability is struck by the lightning-message of inspiration: the symbol, as bearer of divine and ancient meaning, then, is entirely angelic in function, whose visitation is both requested and welcomed by the unshakeable tranquility of the initiate's heart-mind. The key to summoning the symbol-angel is *righteous concentration*—single-minded absorption in *emanating reverence* and, simultaneously, perfectly-focused intent on *Benefiting All at the Same Time*.

This hexagram is paired with its complement, 12, DUALITY.

Hexagram Sequence

After things have remembered the timeless, they focus on the unchanging:
Concentration is dream attention.

Fixation is not concentration, nor is compulsion; nor, habituation; nor obsession. The uninitiated suffer from a twofold difficulty: first, they do not know what concentration is; and, second, they do not know what to concentrate on. The initiated train to develop their capacity to concentrate fully: this begins with cultivating an inner state of unbroken tranquility, waiting reverentially for a spark of inspiration to fall into the stillness and catch fire; this moment is likened to coming across a path suddenly and following it to its end—or coming across a scent and following it to its source. From this perspective, concentration is the capacity to shut out all other things while following one thing in its development and interaction with all other things. For the initiated, moreover, all of Creation is a text of the divine word made flesh—there is nothing that is not a living symbol of the infinite and eternal *One*—and there is nothing more consequential upon which to concentrate than the meaning of symbols, which lead back to the primordial Act of Creation. This is analogous to viewing the most distant stars and interpreting their light as leading back to the beginning of time. The interpretation of living symbols in light of the message they carry from the *One* is the only way in which living beings may understand the correct relationship between themselves and all other beings. The uninitiated forgo this practice and so ignore their own meaning-as-symbol leading back to the *One*—and thereby dwell in ignorance of their true relationship to the *One*. Unbroken concentration on the ever-deepening meaning of every living symbol they encounter, the initiated read the text of Creation and are thereby borne by those messengers back to the source of All.

Mantic Formula

Lightning strikes the mountain summit:
You unite earth and sky.

Dream attention, then, is the truest form of concentration: utterly present amid constantly shifting and unpredictable events arising within the *psychic substance* of the dream—of which the dreamer is an intrinsic part—*dream attention* takes every detail of the dream *as a symbol* linked in a web of living meaning that is coherent not just within the dream, but within the largest possible contexts of the dream. In other words: each of the details of a dream have a meaning; and all of those details together have a meaning; and that collective meaning stands coherent across the entirety of the dream; and *that* collective meaning takes its place within the life of the dreamer, coherent enough to effect attitudes and behaviors in waking life; and those changes in attitudes and behaviors have the potential to effect far larger contexts within social interactions in the world of manifestation; and those changes in attitude and behavior have the potential of effecting Memory and Understanding of the soul and so provoking changes within the pre-manifestation realm; and, so on. *Dream attention* takes every detail of the dream *as a symbol*—this is the test of true concentration: as a living symbol itself within the *psychic substance*, can it interpret every other image within the *psychic substance* as a living symbol bearing its unique meaning-message from the Divine?

As a whole, this formula signifies that you embody *true concentration,* applying the practice of *dream attention* to every moment of experience in every realm of emanation.

INTENT

Bottom Line. Vigilant essence: Humankind changing everything they know about nature.

Second Line. Vigilant essence: Humankind changing everything they know about human nature.

Third Line. Vigilant essence: Humankind changing everything they know about spirit.

Fourth Line. Vigilant essence: Angels' visitations in humankind's dreams.

Fifth Line. Vigilant essence: Angels' visitations in humankind's relationships.

Top Line. Vigilant essence: Angels' visitations in humankind's memories.

52

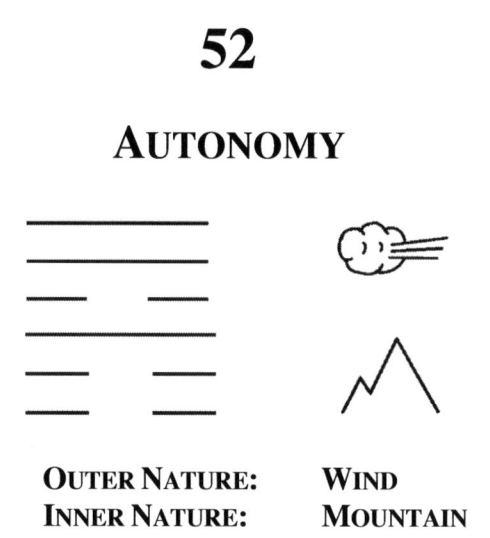

AUTONOMY

| OUTER NATURE: | WIND |
| INNER NATURE: | MOUNTAIN |

Mountain within, Wind without: Incubation within, Adaptation without

Wind outside symbolizes adaptation, while Mountain inside symbolizes stability. Where lightning struck the mountain summit, now wind blows unrestricted across the sky above the mountain. The contraction of awareness down to single-pointed concentration has led to the expansion of awareness across the entire range of existence. The stable, moored sense of self provides a solid foundation for the freedom of spirit neither domesticated by others nor hobbled by fear. The initiated follow the road as far as others have carved it into the landscape—to the edge of the unexplored and unbroken wilderness, the initiated follow the road and then set off on their own to carve their own way. Their own *tao*.

This hexagram is paired with its complement, 11, PROJECTION.

Hexagram Sequence

After things have explored the spirit world, they find their niche:
Autonomy is the immortal spirit body.

Traversing the pre-manifestation realm of the spirit world, the soul comes to name itself. *The soul is a symbol that stands for itself.* The entire course of its beginningless and endless existence is comprised of the act of reading that symbol, of interpreting its own meaning, of coming face-to-face with its own message-as-messenger translating it—the *soul-symbol*—back to the primordial Act of Creation of the *One*. Circumnavigating the interior of the Sphere of Universal Communion, encountering great teachers and allies alike, the initiated come to the realization that they are *reflective* of all other beings but *relative* to the Source from which all originate and to which all return. Such is the root of autonomy, for *experiencing* all other beings as reflective of oneself establishes the deeper reality of one's primary—and, ultimately, only—relationship to the Source of All Creation. Each being, from this stance, perceives every being as a mirror reflecting all other mirrors—each mirror autonomous in its relationship to all other mirrors and their reflections; autonomous, because the true standing of each is its relation to the source of all mirror-beings.

The higher soul and lower soul are yoked and their plowing turns over the ground of being, exposing the fertile soil receptive to the sowing of the seed of the immortal spirit body. Once rooted and cultivated, its branches extend into the invisible, where its single blossom is released to sail forever on the four winds of *The Beyond*.

Mantic Formula

True freedom has no purpose:
You roam free and easy.

Standing on the edge of eternity, the initiated gaze steadfastly into the inner void of their soul, recognizing the perfect reflection cast there in the mirror of the vast Unmanifested. Drifting in the *aware space* of the time both before and after all other beings arise, the initiated come to realize that *every* being is the *first* being—such is the nature of the relationship to the Source of All Creation. Watching the stars being born all at once, one is already ancient; watching the stars blink out one by one, one is reborn. Against the backdrop of eternity, one must be self-governing, already one of the ancestors, walking among the ancient gods and goddesses: where there is no body, there is no gravity; where there is no gravity, there is only flight. *True freedom* is free of everything—free of purpose; free of antipathy; free even of what one reveres. *True autonomy* is the capacity to adapt to one's surroundings free of undue influence from either internal or external compulsions—self-governance, in other words, can only—indeed, *must* only—result in internal and external actions that embody the virtues pronounced by one's *soul-symbol*.

As a whole, this formula signifies that you are an untroubled spirit, passing through lifetimes with grace, trailing in your wake relicts of transcendental beauty.

INTENT

Bottom Line. Surpassing conscience: Harmony with nature being treated as the highest priority.

Second Line. Surpassing conscience: Culture surviving through adaptability, not strength.

Third Line. Surpassing conscience: Identity surviving through metamorphosis, not security.

Fourth Line. Surpassing conscience: Soul surviving through union, not identity.

Fifth Line. Surpassing conscience: Being surviving through nonbeing, not thought.

Top Line. Surpassing conscience: Awareness surviving through space, not time.

53

DISILLUSIONING

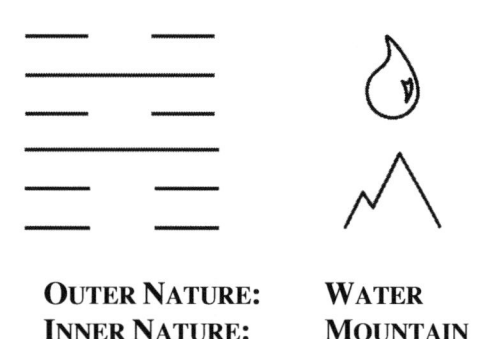

OUTER NATURE: **WATER**
INNER NATURE: **MOUNTAIN**

Mountain within, Water without: Incubation within, Mystery without

Water outside symbolizes the Great Mystery, while Mountain inside symbolizes the retort of distillation. The Great Mystery does not have a human conscience. It helps catalyze within human nature a conscience, but it has no conscience that human nature would ever recognize. If an insect falls into a lake and, despite its struggles, fails to extricate itself and so drowns, the lake feels no remorse nor guilt nor pity—rather, it falls immediately to the task of incorporating the insect's body back into the Whole. So it is with the Great Mystery, for it is not only the womb of creative renewal, but also the tomb of death, of one's own death and the death of all one's loved ones, of all that one ever loved. Authentically encountering the Great Mystery within the manifestation realm draws human nature into the retort of distillation, wherein all its illusions are refined back to original perception. The mountain-retort of alchemical incubation is the lower soul capable of withstanding the spiritual heat of intent that must be applied to the water-mystery if its dregs-illusions are to be refined until they expose its hidden truth.

This hexagram is paired with its complement, 10, PASSION.

Hexagram Sequence

After things have drunk from the oasis, they see through the mirage:
Disillusioning is seeing the world through the soul's eyes.

The uninitiated will witness a shaman or a mystic or a medium entering the other world and say to themselves, *Ah, they are going into a trance.* But the truth of the matter is quite different, for it is *they* who are in a lifelong trance. As to the shaman or mystic or medium, all their training and preparation to enter the other world constitute a practice of *breaking the trance*. Social conditioning, as it has been practiced in this Dark Age, is an act of establishing a universal trance-state that holds human nature in thrall to a consensual worldview dictated by the five senses and their corrupted logic. It is a trance that seeks to weave *spiderwebs over the eyes*, as some ancients have it—an attempt to channel perception of the world away from its underlying reality of the sacredness of all things and toward rationalizations and justifications for the desecration of both nature and human nature. It is not necessary that everyone fall under the spell of the trance all the time in order for it to be effective—it is enough to have the vast majority be under its sway the vast majority of the time, as the social gravity of the worldview pulls the outliers back into the consensus, lulling them back into the sleepwalking state.

The initiated awaken to a living world of miraculous nature and angelic human nature and they do not fall back asleep.

Mantic Formula

The mirror beholds its own image in other mirrors:
You break through the gaze of self.

The soul is a symbol that stands for itself. Within a dream, the soul appears to the other living elements of the dream as its *symbol*, not as its body appears in the manifestation realm. Nor is the soul seeing other beings in the dream as they appear in their manifestation body—it is seeing their *symbols*. This is the great lesson of the initiated: the manifestation bodies of all the beings encountered in one's lifetime are not their true appearances—*true seeing* perceives the *symbol* that *is* each manifestation body, rather than perceiving the manifestation body itself. Even for those with experience in the pre-manifestation realm of the World Soul, this disillusioning requires diligence, as seeing through the mirage of the manifestation realm does not become second nature without sustained effort. Once the symbol perceives itself in the gaze of others, however, the trance is effectively broken forever, as the nature of the symbol's virtues subsumes the life-negating worldview of social conditioning. As a whole, this formula signifies that you see yourself through the eyes of the soul, and the spiderwebs are washed away thereby.

INTENT

Bottom Line. Reverse play: Mind seeing through habit's mirage.

Second Line. Reverse play: The Secret Council steering humankind away from the precipice.

Third Line. Reverse play: The earthen churning pot stirs the Milky Way.

Fourth Line. Reverse play: The Creative Forces and Creative Will marrying to produce dance and song.

Fifth Line. Reverse play: Behind the theater curtain, a second stage and a second production.

Top Line. Reverse play: The inner dragon breathes fire through the eyes.

54

EXTINGUISHING

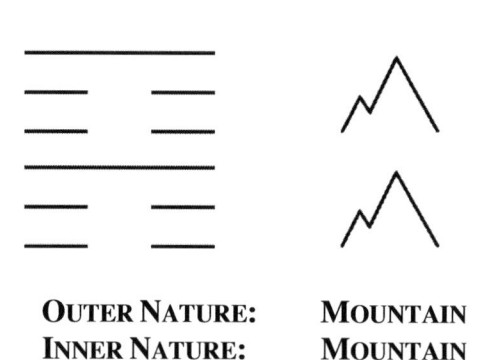

| OUTER NATURE: | MOUNTAIN |
| INNER NATURE: | MOUNTAIN |

Mountain within, Mountain without: Incubation within, Incubation without

Mountain outside symbolizes interruption of external state, while Mountain inside symbolizes interruption of internal state. The unfolding of Creation moves toward Completion; the blossoming of psyche seeds the realm of manifestation. The soul's impetus toward manifestation as a human being is much more complex than with other beings, due to the characteristic of self-awareness within human nature. This aspect is traditionally called *Thinking* and is considered to be the outgrowth of the more primal *Being*—there can be *Being* without *Thinking*, after all, but there cannot be *Thinking* without *Being*. It is axiomatic within the ancients' wisdom teachings that the greater part of the *social trance* of human nature is the result of self-awareness dwelling almost completely in *Thinking* to the near-exclusion of conscious *Being*. *Thinking* is concerned with establishing itself as the subject of awareness and all other things as the object of thought; this duality separates human nature from all other beings, including other human beings, primarily by treating them as concepts within thought as opposed to encountering them directly within the mystical unity of *Being*. Setting itself up at the center of awareness, around which all other things revolve, *Thinking* creates a running commentary on experience, comprised of: memories of past experience; associations with other things; conclusions about the reason things happened or are happening or will happen; judgements about the good and bad of things based on personal preferences; opinions about the right and wrong of things; as well as numerous personal desires and fears colored by an overarching life-mood, such as optimism, pessimism, melancholy, and so on. It is likewise axiomatic among the wisdom teachings that this running commentary constitutes a narrative of the individual's life that comes to take the place of actual experience by so dominating awareness.

Mountain outside disrupts the flow of the narrative about the person's surroundings. Mountain inside disrupts the flow of the narrative about the person's thoughts, emotions, and memories. This twofold interruption of the narrative is the time-proven practice whereby a person's *Thinking* is stopped and awareness reverts full force to *Being*. Mountain inside and outside signifies stopping, reverting to stillness, contemplative quietude.

This hexagram is paired with its complement, 9, IMMERSION.

Hexagram Sequence

After things have seen through the mirage of form, they see through the oasis of the formless: EXTINGUISHING is freedom even from what is most revered.

The mystic is called to the unity of all things, a state of *Being* in which individual awareness reunites with the One Mind—a state that the wisdom teachings have long pointed at by saying, *A drop of water returns to the sea*: the image is that of an individual mind temporarily separated from the One Mind, which once reunited, dissolves back into the Whole, surrendering the sense of individuality to the sense of oneness. For this to occur, the individual *Thinking-narrative* has to be extinguished as certainly as a fire—a fire is either burning or not: extinguishing it means it is no longer burning. For the *Thinking-narrative* to be fully extinguished means awareness stops, reverts to the stillness of *Being* and empties out *all* the contents of thought at once. The practice consists of *turning awareness back onto itself*, making awareness the object of awareness rather than the thinking subject: *aware only of awareness* fuses subject and object into an experiential unity devoid of either subject or object. This is the short path to mystical unity with the One Mind, as *awareness of awareness* leads directly to the source of awareness. Voluntarily extinguishing the sense of individuality automatically cuts off the entire *Thinking-narrative* and all its concepts in a single step, eliminating the need for a long period of self-cultivation before awakening. Few hear the truth and even fewer believe: *if the stream of consciousness is simply interrupted, awakening occurs spontaneously.*

Mantic Formula

Nowhere to go, nowhere to return:
You extinguish death.

If the individual mind is even temporarily interrupted, the One Mind floods in. Yet the One Mind cannot be grasped, cannot be conceived, cannot be turned into another object of *Thinking*. It is the pure, original essence of *Being*, the *living* One Mind emanating all the realms of existence—it is what gives form and characteristics to all things but is devoid of form and characteristics itself. It is a *living presence* that conceives all things and cannot itself be conceived. It is the *stopping place*, mountain after mountain blocking habit mind from advance, an enclosure of mountains surrounding the One Mind and its own symbol, *We Are I Am*. To extinguish the *narrative-trance* and return to pure *Essence* within the world of manifestation is a challenge even for the initiated, so long as they harbor any vestige of selfhood separate from the All—and especially so long as they harbor any distress or unease about their own pure awareness dissolving back into the One Awareness. *Mystical Unity* is individual awareness absorbed by, and identified with, the *living* One Mind. The wisdom teachings make it clear that this metamorphosis can be undertaken at the moment of dying, as one abandons the body and mind, effectively accomplishing the task of extinguishing the *narrative-trance* as one departs the manifestation realm—but the same teachings make it clear that only a small portion of people actually take advantage of the opportunity, overwhelmed as they are with confusion, fear or unconsciousness. This teaching, however, points to the concrete nature of the practice: those who can decisively and sincerely perform the ritual of *deathbed awareness*, actively and purposefully visualizing their dying moments, may find the short path to interrupting the lifelong stream of *trance-narrative* and step back into the *living immortal* awareness of their angelic soul.

As a whole, this formula signifies that you reach the top of the mountain and keep climbing.

INTENT

Bottom Line. Seamless stillness: Night birds have stopped singing, day birds have not yet begun.

Second Line. Seamless stillness: The room without walls.

Third Line. Seamless stillness: The symbol for meaninglessness searches for its other half.

Fourth Line. Seamless stillness: Angels have a memory, but no memories.

Fifth Line. Seamless stillness: No monarch is free during the migration.

Top Line. Seamless stillness: Stopping and resting.

55

RELAXATION

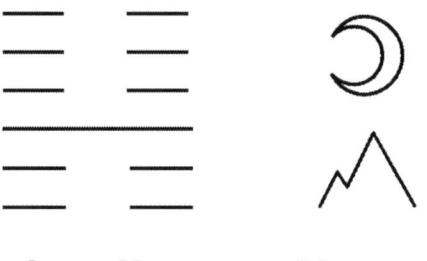

OUTER NATURE: MOON
INNER NATURE: MOUNTAIN

Mountain within, Moon without: Incubation within, Completion without

Moon outside symbolizes completing a cycle, while Mountain inside symbolizes tranquility. The *inner void* transforms human nature, allowing it to return to life in the manifestation realm after its breakthrough in the mystical. The cycle of incubation is complete, its promise fulfilled, and All Creation breathes a sigh of relief. The initiated adhere to the ancients' wisdom teachings: do not presume anything has been attained; that the practice works is no cause to resort to either pride or conceit; step back into the flow of day-to-day life with grace, ease and gratitude; do not speak of the matter until it has had time to ripen; remember that it is the teachings, not the teacher. This phase of the unfolding of Creation permits a restoration of equilibrium now that the interruption in day-to-day awareness has ended—*Thinking* has returned but no longer as master of the house; the transformation has fused it with *Being*, so that the flow of awareness is no longer driven by habit or conditioning, but serves as the basis of refined discernment and rational thought in support of behaviors consistent with treating all beings as divine. Relaxation in this sense means that a period of profound change is followed by a period of restored continuity, albeit evincing a more dynamic and beneficial equilibrium.

This hexagram is paired with its complement, 8, DEVOTION.

Hexagram Sequence

After things have reconciled form and formless, they revere the ordinary:
Relaxation is the open door of welcoming each moment.

Returning to the day-to-day routines of life in the manifestation realm reminds the initiated to hold each moment sacred, no less significant in the course of eternity than the primordial Act of Creation itself—of which, each is a message echoing the longing howls of mountain wolves beneath the full moon. The ordinary is of a sudden miraculous, routine a source of constant surprise, the world of nature and human nature a font of magical coincidences. The symbol that is the essence of each manifestation shines through its appearance as naturally and spontaneously as the moon coming out from behind clouds. Life takes on greater meaning, anxiety evaporates, time slows to a standstill in the present moment. One moves calmly, without hurry or wasted effort, relieved of burdens and preoccupation. Experience passes through one, like sunlight through a magnifying glass: momentous effects issue from innocent actions. Without striving, one acts like a force of nature itself—the breeze winds up the ravine in the morning and down the ravine in the evening, the tides turn with the moon and the seasons with the sun, cicadas wait for decades underground before emerging to mate, a mother soothes her infant before it cries. No deliberation, no arguing with oneself about possible decisions and outcomes. One strolls along a wide open beach, past one good omen after another.

Mantic Formula

Deathless, stranger to fear:
You open your soul to all.

What is left of the extinguishing phase? Just this *presence* of the immortal being at the core of awareness. This living being shines through the clouds of human nature, suddenly *here*, like the moon really seen for the first time, when it had always been *there*. The first-hand experience of one's immortality is like an earthquake casting down cities and overturning mountains: the unconscious fear of death—one's own and one's loved ones'—so long a fixture in the firmament of one's vision of inevitable night, comes crashing down like a rain of constellations to reveal the pure, transparent radiance of eternal life ever shining behind the curtain of the five senses. All Creation breathes a sigh of relief. Nothing obstructing the way, lifetimes to complete the work. The body relaxes into deathlessness.

As a whole, this formula signifies that you drop your guard on every front and let it all flood in.

INTENT

Bottom Line. Tranquil comfort: Fire in the fireplace, water in the well.

Second Line. Tranquil comfort: Perfect harmony between society and the individual.

Third Line. Tranquil comfort: A generation of humankind who have completed their work.

Fourth Line. Tranquil comfort: The passing storm leaves bright calm in its wake.

Fifth Line. Tranquil comfort: The need for distractions passes, leaving bright calm in its wake.

Top Line. Tranquil comfort: The mind flower dwells in the heart of the mountain.

56

RECAPITULATION

OUTER NATURE: SUN
INNER NATURE: MOON

Moon within, Sun without: Completion within, Creation without

Sun outside symbolizes the beginning of a cycle, while Moon inside symbolizes the completion of a cycle. As the unfolding of Creation nears Completion, it arrives at this phase of the *embodied microcosm*. The movement of *psyche* into manifestation contracts again, following the wide-open expansion of Relaxation. This is a profound contraction, however, as unimaginable as the contraction of a great oak into its acorn— but not just a single acorn, for the oak's ritual is one of producing an entire generation of offspring every cycle. Each acorn, a perfect replication of the oak, yet each a different manifestation according to the circumstances into which they fall: this one lands in a wide open meadow and so grows straight and tall, coming to dominate the entire meadow; that one lands on the ledge of a rocky cliff and so grows twisted and gnarled, its roots holding back the exposed rocks of the cliff face. Identical in essence, cast from the same source in the same generation, yet utterly different in form dependent on lived experiences. *As Above, So Below*: All Creation periodically contracts in the same manner, producing an entire generation of *embodied microcosms* of its alive and aware *Being*. This *outflux* of divine nature emanates through the souls of *pure intent* and into their manifestation bodies. This is a profound contraction, though, because it produces individuals whose ego-identities have already been stilled and whose heart-minds have already taken up the practice of welcoming all in: what floods in is All Creation, recapitulating the whole of its unfolding in the form of awakened human nature. Identical in essence, cast from the same source in the same generation, yet each *being* unique in its manifestation of enlightenment depending on circumstances and lived experiences.

This hexagram is paired with its complement, 7, ORIENTATION.

HEXAGRAM SEQUENCE

After things have opened their hearts to All, they repeat the cycle of death and rebirth:
RECAPITULATION is the time between lives.

The body awakens to *the Imaginal*. This is to say that the *embodied microcosm* no longer perceives just the manifestation realm—it wakes as if from a dream to find itself in the miraculous ocean of circulating *creative intent* that hitherto has only been experienced as the *psychic substance* of the pre-manifestation realm of the World Soul. The living macrocosm, the *One*, recapitulates itself in the awakened individual, whose perceptions are no longer restricted to the five senses and whose cognition is no longer restricted to the human orbit. It is not just the World Soul that is suddenly perceptible, in other words, but the *Ideas* of the Pure Mind realm just as spontaneously burst afire with the divine light of the archangels' names. The body awakens to *Dreamtime*—the manifestation body is spontaneously transformed into the dream body, able to penetrate the veils between the realms of emanation. For the *embodied microcosm*, there are no barriers within the single *living emanation* of the *One*: it moves through the spirit world even as it moves through the manifestation world, it moves through the realm of the One Memory even as it moves through the realm of the One Mind—occupying all the open spaces between things, it continuously works to re-form the relationships binding and unbinding things in their evolving reflection of Beauty, Truth and Harmony. Ending cycles, beginning cycles—it is all the sacred circle of death and rebirth: herein is the mystic seed produced between every life, between every generation, the roots of which evolve to knot time into eternity.

Mantic Formula

Descending the ladder to ascend:
You rediscover purpose in the soul's lifetime.

Creation summons itself. Here is the evocation that the initiated long to witness, for it represents the turning point in the culmination of the journey to Completion. Impossible for the uninitiated to imagine: who first extinguishes *everything* and then welcomes *everything* in? Only the living *One*; and its *embodied microcosm*. The *One* must contract down into an individual manifestation of its own living presence periodically in order to consciously and fully experience its Creation *from the inside*. The individual manifestation serves, then, as the divine mortal eyes and hands of the divine immortal, incarnated again to unite heaven and earth, to balance and harmonize the visible and invisible realms. Every generation, the *embodied microcosms* make their way through the world of manifestation, fusing moments of *pure idea* and *psychic substance* into the materiality of nature and human nature. Embodied in order to rend the veil of time and draw eternity down into the world of history—and the world of history up into the mind of eternity—such individuals are the very recapitulations of Immortal Wisdom: as such, they require no recognition nor do they avoid it if thrust upon them, for all that matters to them is their work. In this embodied form, the mystic is transformed into an icon of action in the world, even when those actions are imperceptible and anonymous. As a whole, this formula signifies that your work is itself a recapitulation of the primordial Act of Creation and Completion.

INTENT

Bottom Line. River source: Building the first city around a sacred temple deifying a secret wellspring.

Second Line. River source: Freedom of expression and action in an enlightened civilization.

Third Line. River source: Living the mythic life of free and easy wandering.

Fourth Line. River source: Avoiding the trap of enlightenment, the soul soars between heaven and earth.

Fifth Line. River source: Ever returning to the basics of love for all life and generosity of spirit.

Top Line. River source: The eternal mind-moment is one of unbroken awe and wonder.

57

CONSECRATION

OUTER NATURE:	LAKE
INNER NATURE:	MOON

Moon within, Lake without: Completion within, Wonder without

Lake outside symbolizes joyous communion, while Moon inside symbolizes completion of a cycle. The unfolding of Creation aims at the full realization of potential at the most concrete level. Within the manifestation realm, the profound contraction of Recapitulation is followed by an equally profound expansion in the phase of Consecration—the *awakened body* re-enters day-to-day life with a fuller sense of the sacredness of everything. It is a complex transition, for on the surface nothing has changed in the world; but for the *returnee*, the whole of the world has taken on a new cast—one of *lushness*, an emotional radiance pouring from every *thing*, every *being*, every *part*: where once spirit poured through matter, now matter pours through spirit in the absolute materialization of soul. The *returnee* has become the *real person*, who consciously realizes the primordial imagination as a sense organ.

This hexagram is paired with its complement, 6, CULTIVATION.

HEXAGRAM SEQUENCE

After things have reawakened the immortal within, they treat everything as sacred:
CONSECRATION is divinity recognizing divinity.

Comes the *consecration of the individual*—consciously accepting one's own sacred nature, one's own divinity, is an act of sanctifying the individual life, the mortal soul, that has been raised up by the phase of Recapitulation. It is like stepping into a role in a sacred play, like accepting the mantle of an archetype: embodying the divinity emanated by the *One* is not, however, a matter of the *intention* of the Poetic Imagination to *project* its soul-symbol—rather, it is a matter of the Receptive Imagination, that most primary of the sensory organs, *perceiving* its true nature. This act of conscious receptivity of one's own sacred nature cannot be attained by conceptual means—it is entirely nonconceptual and has no entryway but through one's own transcendent individuality: it is impossible to suddenly be immersed in the divinity of All without spontaneously recognizing one's own divinity. This state is amplified by one's interactions with everything one encounters: the divinity of each being—whether a leaf, a cloud, a raindrop, an ocean, an insect, a cat, another human being, and so on—is a palpable *presence* as resonant as a bell-struck tone permeating all other beings. Including oneself. For these tones ring from every thing, resonating in subtle harmonies that reinforce the divine nature of each. Harmonies that echo with one's own tone.

MANTIC FORMULA

The center is everywhere:
You are welcomed into Eden.

The *real person* stands ever at the center of reality. This is the divinized individual, one whose humility is strong enough to bear the symbol of its being—and unself-conscious enough to bear the gaze of all other divine beings. Paradoxically, the result of this transcendental leap into the angelomorphic state is to make the individual *more human*. It is true that the inhumane aspects of human nature could be said to justify a cold embrace of emotional distancing from the heavens, but the most sublime sensitivities of the divine heart only ring with deep compassion and empathy for the lostness and alienation most of the uninitiated experience in their day-to-day lives—how much more so for the vulnerable animals, plants and habitats. The center of reality ever stands on the site of the *awakened heart*: there is no source of joyous communion more sublime or concrete than Universal Love, nor is there a greater source of human benevolence than the *real person* embodying the divine solely for the benefit of the world of manifestation. As a whole, this formula signifies that you have stepped back into the time before the initial wound, back into the time of the primordial Act of Creation, where divine breath first became flesh and divine voice first became soul.

INTENT

Bottom Line. Birthright ecstasy: A community gathers in torchlight to welcome a new member.

Second Line. Birthright ecstasy: One hundred generations of Holy Peace.

Third Line. Birthright ecstasy: A comet returns to visit the dreams of the whole world.

Fourth Line. Birthright ecstasy: The yoke of immortality.

Fifth Line. Birthright ecstasy: The angels themselves revering humankind's art.

Top Line. Birthright ecstasy: The divine child teaches an assembly of ancient gods and goddesses.

58

CONFORMITY

OUTER NATURE: FIRE
INNER NATURE: MOON

Moon within, Fire without: Completion within, Knowledge without

Fire outside symbolizes cultivation, while Moon inside symbolizes completion of a cycle. The difficulty that the modern mind faces upon awakening is the lack of a tradition that carries the individual through the reintegration with human nature and into the role of authentic transmission of the lamp. By tradition, the time period for such reintegration is thirty years—a symbolic number, to be sure, but one that slows down the tendency to begin speaking right away about what one has experienced. Indeed, it is axiomatic among the wisest that, *Once awake, you begin teaching where you left off in the last life*—unaware, at first, how much the world of manifestation has changed between lives, one reflexively takes up the teachings as if no time has passed. Beyond that, the *real person* must adapt to the individual human nature of the body with which it now associates, making use of its experiences to draw the teachings closer to the needs of the uninitiated. For these reasons, what is called for is *Conformity* with the traditional practice of cultivating enlightenment.

This hexagram is paired with its complement, 5, INTERPRETATION.

Hexagram Sequence

After things have accepted their angelic nature, they move between identities at will:
Conformity is soul taking on the form given it.

The overall purpose of the cultivation is the *return to normalcy*. By *normal* is meant the original nature of radiant awareness in its state of pure Being, uncontrived by the instincts or social conditioning of the manifestation body. The first transmission of the teachings is, then, to the manifestation body, especially as regards its habitual responses to the world based upon its instincts and conditioning. The integration with the body does not eradicate the instincts or conditioning—it frees the body of compulsive reactions to its surroundings. This allows the body, likewise, to return to normalcy, as an adapted being with the widest range of potential responses to circumstances. At the same time, the body's experiences and memories are being assimilated in order to form a coherent and accurate vision of the historical epoch in which one finds oneself—this aspect of cultivation is necessary if the wisdom teachings are to be adapted in a meaningful way to one's contemporaries. Water takes the form given it: poured into a jar, it takes the form of a jar; poured into the ocean, it takes the form of the sea. Enlightened awareness is like this, too.

Mantic Formula

The ordinary is miraculous:
You avoid all trappings of specialness.

Don't speak too soon—until fully acquainted with the times, you will simply repeat universals that can be gleaned from many sources. To be of benefit to specific needs, you require spending time serving other beings' needs, be they human, animal, plant or the wider world of nature. This extended time in service is thought of as *dwelling on the mountainside*, as in a hermitage: leaving yourself alone, you attend to the needs of others and, through diligence, refine your understanding of the times and your own skillful means of responding to its needs. In this way, you bring eternal wisdom into accord with human nature and universal compassion into accord with lived experience. Above all, the return to normalcy means that you are fully aware that the awakened state is the natural evolution of consciousness and, hence, nothing exceptional. As a whole, this formula signifies that you cultivate true dignity and humility while placing all others above you.

INTENT

Bottom Line. Ceremonial duty: Souls returning from the dead as hummingbirds to encourage the living.

Second Line. Ceremonial duty: Weighed at death, the heart is lighter than a feather.

Third Line. Ceremonial duty: Upon meeting, souls exchanging memories unconsciously.

Fourth Line. Ceremonial duty: The path to Completion runs through the land of forgetting.

Fifth Line. Ceremonial duty: Upon meeting, souls exchanging understanding unconsciously.

Top Line. Ceremonial duty: On a moonless night, a thunderbolt lights the entire terrain forever.

59

INSPIRATION

OUTER NATURE: LIGHTNING
INNER NATURE: MOON

Moon within, Lightning without: Completion within, Motivation without

Lightning outside symbolizes surprise, while Moon inside symbolizes completion of a cycle. Within the unfolding of Creation, the phase of *Conformity* shapes the individual to the ever-flowing current of the Imaginal, transforming them into a source of *Inspiration* for others. The initiated are not primarily in accord with people based on their words—it is, rather, their *presence* that attracts their attention and draws them into collaborative alliances. The uninitiated respond to others in exactly the same way on an unconscious level but too often allow their innate sensitivities to be overridden by their susceptibility to convincing speech. Because of their conformity to true normalcy, the *real person* is like an upside-down person to much of the manifestation realm: their presence is palpable as a kind of charisma, an invisible magnetism drawing the visible into accord with the intent of the *One*. What they do, how they do it, what they do not do, why they do not do it—all their reasons and priorities seem to the uninitiated like the view of a person upside-down to the world. But to the initiated, especially, they are a source of inspiration marking out the overgrown path of freedom, love and beauty.

This hexagram is paired with its complement, 4, RECOGNITION.

Hexagram Sequence

After things have become anything, they become the teachings themselves:
INSPIRATION is omnipresent Grace.

The capacity of enlightened awareness to take on any form in conformity with the wisdom teachings means that it comes now to take on the form of the teachings themselves—spoken and unspoken, remembered and forgotten, revealed and hidden: no conscious learning compasses the whole of the teachings, but they *can* be embodied. *Eternal Wisdom* is the individual embodiment of the teachings; it is neither abstract nor impersonal. It is the *real person* who steps into manifestation and, in the most spontaneous and least contrived manner, emanates *divine grace*, a felt presence radiating from within but effecting all nearby—an *angelic charisma* overflowing the body and inspiring all it touches to aspire to the fullest realization, and highest expression, of freedom, love and beauty. To inspire others is to be inspired by the ever-surprising manner in which the manifestation realm reveals its living symbols to its own embodied spirit—as its interpretations become more metaphorical, its symbols become more literal, assuming a concreteness mirroring that of dew on the hourglass, the obsidian cradle of the ancient gods and goddesses, the rainbow bridge connecting heaven and earth: spoken and unspoken, remembered and forgotten, revealed and hidden, *Eternal Wisdom* ever surprises itself.

Mantic Formula

The all-at-onceness of the realized world:
You draw the dream up close around you.

The teachings are clear in regard to expressing the miraculous nature of Life: *Do what is beautiful.* Not beautiful, of course, by others' standards, but by one's own interpretation of the *presence behind absence*. Within the world of manifestation, it is the absence of things—loved ones, security, certainty, meaning, companionship, equality, ease, justice, harmony and balance with the natural world, and so on—that detracts from human happiness and leads to feelings of helplessness, hopelessness and meaninglessness. The *real person*, however, sees in each of these absences the symbol of their *longing* for the sense of *Belonging to the Whole*—and herein lies *The Beautiful*: it is the body's sense of exile in an inhuman universe that reveals the soul's quintessential sense of homesickness that thereby makes evident the trans-lifetime memory of the *Universal Homecoming*. Within every instance of absence, in other words, there dwells its complementary symbol of the living presence of the *Return to the Act of Creation*—a living symbol of presence arising from the transformation of its correlative symbol of absence. For the initiated, this is an act of worship, releasing the light from its spell of darkness, thereby providing inspiration for others to authentically witness the *living perfection* within which they eternally exist. As a whole, this formula signifies that you do not fall even into the present moment, avoiding thereby creating the illusion of past and future—rather, you maintain your conscious connection to the World Soul, swaddling yourself in the blissful intent of its *psychic substance*.

INTENT

Bottom Line. Spirit breath: Great-souled allies changing the course of a broken river.

Second Line. Spirit breath: The World Soul abides as an ancient alchemical laboratory.

Third Line. Spirit breath: Fully awakened individuals manifesting change independently.

Fourth Line. Spirit breath: The victorious ones shining like a signal fire on the mountaintop.

Fifth Line. Spirit breath: Rituals honoring the lives of the dead and the not-yet-living.

Top Line. Spirit breath: Humility expressed as maintaining the practice to the end.

60

IDENTIFICATION

OUTER NATURE: WIND
INNER NATURE: MOON

Moon within, Wind without: Completion within, Adaptation without

Wind outside symbolizes adaptation, while Moon inside symbolizes completion of a cycle. First, *Form adores Form*. Then, *Form adores the Formless*. Finally, *the Formless adores Form*. Spirit adapts, in the end, to its destined manifestation—not out of inevitability, although it is inevitable, but out of adoration, reverence and communion. Formless awareness identifies with the body's form in a conscious and purposeful act of uniting the higher soul with the lower soul in the most profound manner: *angelic being* identifies with *human nature,* finding therein its mystical marriage with *The Beloved*. This inevitable identification with the body is the result of a *soul pact* one makes with oneself in the World Soul prior to ever taking form in the manifestation realm—prior, even, to the emanation of the manifestation realm itself. All one's life, the body has, unawares, looked through the soul's eyes, but from this point forward the soul looks through the body's eyes. This is, of course, a matter of mutual adoration, for the *angelic being* is The Beloved of the body's lower soul, as well. That this union occurs before the body's death is significant, since it produces a divine child, the *immortal spirit body*, which has the capacity to *influence the manifestation realm directly with its intent*—prior to this phase of realization, the soul is able to influence the manifestation realm indirectly, solely via its intent in the pre-manifestation realm.

This hexagram is paired with its complement, 3, INTENTION.

Hexagram Sequence

After things have become a font of renewal, they accept their unborn nature:
IDENTIFICATION is pouring water into water.

An essential turning point of the practice comes when the individual mind identifies with the One Mind; this allows the individual mind to expand beyond the limits of its past experience of self and incorporate the timeless thoughts and memories of the ancient savants. The current phase of unfolding mirrors that important transformation, in that it marks the coming of an age when the One Mind identifies with the individual mind; this allows Universal Thought to contract down to the moment-by-moment lived intent of *transmuted mortality*—uncreated and unborn awareness pours into individual mind like wind into an empty room; and pours out again. *Inspiration* illumines and *Identification* rises to meet it in reflection, divinity pouring into divinity, water into water, essence into essence: now every thought is an image of the divine word, a sacred symbol uttered by living light and echoed in the endless cavern of individual mind—echoing in the emptiness, divine thought doubled back onto itself and doubled again, immortal spirit crystalized into mortal intent and reflected back out into the fertile spatiality of living night like the moon throwing back the sun's light into the poet's eyes, the lover's heart and the ocean's tide. Now the timeless thoughts and memories of the ancient savants whirlwind their dancing way beneath the desert moon, coalescing, gathering momentum and casting its own wind, its own timeless intent, into the fertile spatiality of living time.

Mantic Formula

The North Star changes place:
You align yourself to the true heading.

An essential turning point in the practice comes when individual intent identifies with Universal Intent; this allows the soul's concerns to be intensified by the Universal Good, thereby entering the *sphere of change* in the manifestation realm. The current phase of unfolding mirrors that important transformation, in that it marks the coming of an age when Universal Intent identifies with individual intent; this allows

Universal Good to contract down to the moment-by-moment lived *absences and the presence behind them*—to experience the concerns of mortality while having recourse to change circumstances directly within the world of manifestation. At first, the lower soul identifies with the manifestation body, which limits participation in the world; next, the lower soul identifies with the higher soul, which indirectly expands participation in the world; finally, the higher soul identifies with the manifestation body, which establishes direct participation in the world. This follows the ancient adage, *What one identifies with, becomes one*. In this sense, much of the ancient wisdom teachings elicit a practice of identifying with progressively higher spiritual realities. As a whole, this formula signifies that you take great comfort in knowing that there is ever a higher reality.

INTENT

Bottom Line. Facing mirrors: Medicines pour forth from nature in unending blessings.

Second Line. Facing mirrors: Nature pantomimes its intentions, needs and wishes.

Third Line. Facing mirrors: A symbol dreams itself.

Fourth Line. Facing mirrors: The drop embodies the ocean.

Fifth Line. Facing mirrors: The drop leaves the ocean to embody the raincloud.

Top Line. Facing mirrors: The drop embodies streams and rivers rushing to rejoin the ocean.

61

INTEGRITY

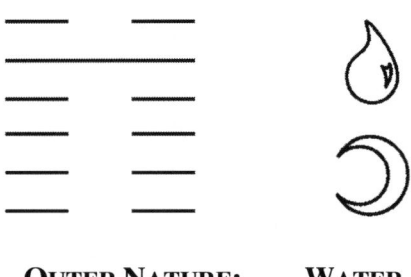

OUTER NATURE: **WATER**
INNER NATURE: **MOON**

Moon within, Water without: Completion within, Mystery without

Water outside symbolizes the Great Mystery, while Moon inside symbolizes realization of potential. As Creation nears the end of its unfolding, it expands to encompass and integrate the objective and subjective, the absolute and relative, the universal and individual. All Creation is, certainly, a non-duality; yet, that non-duality consists on each and every level of a duality comprised of complementary forces responsible for the continuing creating and sustaining of the emanations of the *One*. The invisible and visible are fused into a non-duality, like every other pair of complements, in the furnace of fate. First, the timing: it can only occur when the *being* has realized its full potential. Second, the catalyst: it requires an authentic encounter with the Unknown. It is not enough, in other words, to complete the work of the self-liberation practice—the *being* must, with full faculties human and divine, step into the abyss of the Great Mystery and engage the utterly Unknown.

This hexagram is paired with its complement, 2, FOREKNOWLEDGE.

Hexagram Sequence

After things have transcended every semblance, they achieve true coherence:
INTEGRITY is the indivisibility of intent.

This phase of the unfolding allows for the further unfolding of Creation. A realized *being*, with full faculties human and divine, including the intuition to anticipate coming change, is completely prepared for any eventuality, and so is in harmonious equilibrium with All Creation. But the full realization of potential runs the risk of stalling the momentum of the *continuing creation* by maintaining the present direction of the unfolding. The arising of The Unknown, given the nature of the living *being*, creates *new horizons*, as the encounter with the Great Mystery pushes the boundaries of Creation further into the yet-to-be-known: it is the *being-without-boundaries* who, in investigating The Unknown, opens the gate to new vistas of Creation. This is to say, that the individual embodying Creation extends the unfolding of Creation. Herein lies the secret of *sacred integrity*, for in the end, it is the Whole that enters into the Part in order to instill in the Whole, from within the Whole, the seed of the further unfolding of the Whole. It is this *original intent*, essentialized in every Part, that binds the Whole in an indivisible unity that includes, paradoxically, its own unknowable unfolding.

Mantic Formula

A monkey touches the moon's reflection in the pond:
The moon trembles in its orbit.

Sitting around the campfire, the old ones hear strange growls in the night, see glinting eyes and flashing fangs in the firelight—a wolf pack, brazen, circling the camp in a concerted probing curiosity, drawn by the smell of the day's catch. But the ancestors do not react fearfully. Or aggressively. Instead, they toss small scraps of food out onto the edge of the firelight, inviting the most intelligent and daring to come forward, bit by bit, closer to their benefactors. Night by night, the ritual is enacted, the ancients engage the dark with calm confidence in their resources, as well as real curiosity as to what their experiment with the pack might produce. This is the same manner in which the *embodied microcosm* encounters and approaches The Unknown.

As a whole, this formula signifies that you unite within yourself the visible and invisible halves of Creation, become the *living intent* of the Great Mystery itself.

INTENT

Bottom Line. Light double: Nature holds its immortality, renewing the whole by allowing parts to die.

Second Line. Light double: Invariable change deters stagnation.

Third Line. Light double: Every number is a symbol.

Fourth Line. Light double: The heart of heaven is the same as the heart of earth.

Fifth Line. Light double: Manifestation body and archangel reunited at the end of the road.

Top Line. Light double: The language of time is images.

62

DISSOLVING

OUTER NATURE:	MOUNTAIN
INNER NATURE:	MOON

Moon within, Mountain without: Completion within, Incubation without

Mountain outside symbolizes interruption, while Moon inside symbolizes completion of a cycle. The ancients had a way of teaching, saying, *One is All, All are One*—what place is there to insert a hair, a knife blade, a thought? Like an impenetrable mountain, such a statement stands inviolable and sacrosanct, the center of the world, around which all orbits in spheres of harmonic meanings. The most potent of solvents, it is the counter-spell to strip every sleight-of-hand illusion from the stage of perception. At the widest-open expansion of Creation's unfolding into The Unknown, no apparition of fear, doubt or unease clouds the vision of the human host: the rising sun dispels the morning mist. *Innate perfectibility* arrives neither through action nor stillness, but through dissolving everything left in the wake of the *vanguard angelic*: ever at the edge of Creation, washing away the footprints directly behind, already in front of the present moment—how the modern mind forgets, *nothing except mind can be conceived*. It shapeshifts into the *oncoming wind*, but from where does it blow? *Integrity* brings all things together in the Grand Unity so It might leapfrog over Itself, while *Dissolving* contracts to the culmination of the thirty years' practice, completely disgorging the contents of past-mind to make clear passage for the onrushing *not-yet-here*. Likewise, *Integrity* draws together all threads into the tapestry of individual wholeness, human and divine, while *Dissolving* contracts to the erasure of individuality and the return of awareness to *original mind*.

This hexagram is paired with its complement, 1, REVELATION.

Hexagram Sequence

After things have attained utmost synthesis, they surrender individuality:
Dissolving is the cloud evaporating into the sky.

Upon hearing the words, *One Mind*, a person ought to awaken immediately. There is nothing holding one back from voluntarily shedding body and mind. There is nothing holding anything together or taking anything apart, nothing coming in and nothing going out: the ventriloquist's dummy and the ventriloquist both refusing to go onstage again—the celestial audience applauds as one. Straddling the visible and invisible realms, the fully-realized individual does not stop there—the Work is about the unfolding of Creation and *that* is the path, the *Tao*, that one sees to the end. *Dissolving* simply means that there was not this thing at one time and it is natural and correct that there not be this thing again—there was a clear sky without clouds, then a cloud arose and drifted across the sky for a while, and then the cloud grew thinner and thinner until it dissolved back into the clear sky: nothing came and nothing left. An ocean swell arises on the surface of the sea in a rolling motion that eventually breaks, collapsing back into the ocean: individual mind arises in the midst of the One Mind, is transported between lands, eventually falling back into the One Mind—it was never separate in the first place. Nothing, in truth, is actually dissolved except perception—lest it be forgotten again: *nothing except mind can be conceived*. In the end, *Dissolving* itself is dissolved, along with all accomplishments and memories: how is it any different than climbing into one's own bed and falling gratefully asleep?

Mantic Formula

The raging stream is finally dammed:
You break the flow.

A mirage is a real thing—it is just not what it appears to be. It appears to be an oasis but it is actually an optical illusion generated by heat waves. It is, however, a real thing. Most of the illusions human nature pursues are real things—they are just not what they appear to be. The same is true of souls: many of the things they pursue are real, but not what they believe them to be—this is the reason that war, poverty, hatred, greed, injustice and the desecration of nature and human nature exist in the manifestation world.

Though individuals assume they accurately perceive the world around them, there is simply too much information for the human nervous system to assimilate in its totality—it is like a raging river that overwhelms everything in its path. This stream of inflowing perception has to be stopped, in the same way that the outflow of *Thinking* has to be stopped. If the unfolding of Creation is to be fully realized, then the *sensorium of perception* needs to be not just an empty stage, but an empty theater, as well. It is in this phase of the unfolding that the mirror of the *Original Imagination* shines, its reflection empty of the *ice within fire* glowing before it.

As a whole, this formula signifies that you return with buoyant anticipation to gentle, dreamless sleep, knowing you will wake again.

INTENT

Bottom Line. Inner void: All of nature is a chrysalis from which the magical transfiguration emerges.

Second Line. Inner void: The Great Work is nothing less than stopping the world for one mind-moment.

Third Line. Inner void: Individuality is the reward for sloughing off individuality.

Fourth Line. Inner void: Great-souled beings eschewing all trappings of enlightenment.

Fifth Line. Inner void: The Shadow of Death is Eternal Life.

Top Line. Inner void: Washing a mud ball.

63

COMPLETION

OUTER NATURE:	MOON
INNER NATURE:	MOON

Moon within, Moon without: Completion within, Completion without

Moon outside symbolizes completion of creation, while Moon inside symbolizes completion of creation. The *Seed of Creation* completes its unfolding, manifesting its original intent in the *Fruit of Completion*. Through every phase of unfolding, it explores the Eternal Pathway from the supernatural to the natural, from divine intent to mortal manifestation, from the *One* to the *Many*. Creation comes to full blossom in Completion—the grandeur and scope of its *universal reach* finding its full realization in the *individual life*. The Pathway is one of sheer diversity, lest any possibility of *the ecstatic* remain unexplored—for, in the end, it is the mortal manifestation, the single individual of the *Many*, that is, miraculously, the *Fruit of Completion* now containing the new *Seed of Creation*.

This hexagram is paired with its complement, 0, CREATION.

Hexagram Sequence

After things have fulfilled their destiny, they return to the beginning:
COMPLETION is the full moon reflecting the sun.

The *innate perfectibility* of all *beings* finds its inevitable actuality in the *sphere of change*, wherein, despite the deficiencies of particular individuals at particular times, the collective interaction of the *Many* results in the moment-to-moment perfection of the Whole. This hidden aspect of human life, handed down in the wisdom teachings of the ancients, is the secret key to unlocking contentment and fulfillment in the world of manifestation. Despite being filled, as it is, with the mirages of imperfection, the manifestation world provides the individual with the refuge of perfection by dint of its participation in the perfection of the Whole. This final phase of the unfolding, in truth, defines the actuality of *perfection*, which ceases to be a state to be attained and becomes an act of change moving in the direction of fully-realized potential. The individual, with full faculties human and divine, consciously steps back into the flow of time to take up a lifeway guided by the ancient dictum, *Awaken Early, Find Lifelong Allies*. Like a carrier of a beneficial contagious virus, the individual arrives at this phase to enjoy the rewards of the practice and implement the benevolent intent of the soul and its alliance. Superficially, the individuals completing their Work in this phase appear to be living ordinary lives—loving loved ones, pursuing passions, working, playing, resting, much like their neighbors. But, beneath the surface of their lifetime, whether standing, sitting, lying down, or walking, they are the fusion of a living human being and an eternal angel—the fusion, in which there are not two but a single *being*. It is all as ordinary as the full moon reflecting the sun's light, yet, for the initiated, there is no greater day-to-day miracle.

The initiated rise in the morning, enjoy their breakfast, plan their day, go about their routines, encourage their loved ones, fulfill their responsibilities, indulge their hobbies, laugh and cry, smile and frown, take no offense and give no offense, enjoy the company of others in public, retire in privacy, relax, and sleep. Such is the behavior of human nature—yet, at the same time, the initiated are also continuing their practice of furthering the *Living Creation*, salvaging nature and human nature from civilization's long-standing propensity toward desecration and contributing their own unique creative works to the benefit of All. For above and beyond everything, the initiated follow the ancients' wisdom teachings: *the enlightenment one seeks does not enter from without—it flows out of one's own heart to encompass All Creation*.

Mantic Formula

Every thousand years, this vine produces a single fruit:
You contain the next generation's seed.

The drive of Creation is not a universe, but an individual completely in harmony and balance with the visible and invisible. This inevitably encompasses the matter of death, which also has been the object of the ancients' wisdom teachings. *Every thing, every being, is perfect in the moment—perfect in the manner of a flower in full bloom. Yet that blossom in its fullness is already fading, already dying, already a harbinger of its own death. All things are perfect as they are experienced, yet they are approaching death: only the initiated heart-mind can authentically contain these two archetypal emotions at the same time— the awe and wonder at the perfection of Creation, and the grief and heartache that all one loves must inevitably die.* This living truth extends to the individual's life, as well, for the profundity of awe and wonder of Creation is matched by the grief and heartache of having to inevitably leave such perfection.

The initiated act as though they are the first human beings. The first angels. The first thoughts. The first souls. They approach life and time and eternity as if exploring uncharted territory and discovering an unknown world. They create, they invent, their own lives because they have discovered this fundamental truth: *the first enlightened person had no predecessor, no teacher and no teaching.* The fully-realized individual, knotting the cord running from Creation to Completion, is not the exception but, rather, the inevitable.

As a whole, this formula signifies that you stop here to knot the cord binding Completion back to Creation.

INTENT

Bottom Line. Full moon: Nature breaks free of its egg and takes wing into the Night.

Second Line. Full moon: The phases of Creation wax and wane with the rise and fall of breath.

Third Line. Full moon: Full circle, laughing out loud.

Fourth Line. Full moon: All of Creation an intoxicating sip of the archangels' elixir.

Fifth Line. Full moon: All of Creation fused in a seamless sphere of Light.

Top Line. Full moon: All of Creation transmuted into the golden flower of Completion.

The Hexagram Chart—

Upper → Lower ↓	☷	☳	☵	☱	☶	☲	☴	☰
☷	9	10	12	15	8	11	13	14
☳	17	18	20	23	16	19	21	22
☵	33	34	36	39	32	35	37	38
☱	57	58	60	63	56	59	61	62
☶	1	2	4	7	0	3	5	6
☲	25	26	28	31	24	27	29	30
☴	41	42	44	47	40	43	45	46
☰	49	50	52	55	48	51	53	54

Locate the hexagram number at the intersection of its upper and lower trigrams

The School of Rational Mysticism

The Toltec I Ching
   with Martha Ramirez-Oropeza

In the Oneness of Time: The Education of a Diviner

Way of the Diviner

When You Catch the Fish, Throw Away the Net: An Autobibliography

RESEARCHES ON THE TOLTEC I CHING:

   Vol. 1. *I Ching Mathematics: The Science of Change*

   Vol. 2 *The Image and Number Treatise: The Oracle and the War on Fate*

   Vol. 3. *The Forest of Fire Pearls Oracle: The Medicine Warrior I Ching*

   Vol. 4. *I Ching Mathematics for the King Wen Version*

   Vol. 5. *Why Study the I Ching? A Brief Course in the Direct Seeing of Reality*

   Vol. 6. *The Open Secret I Ching: The Diviner's Journey and the Road of Freedom*

   Vol. 7. *The Alchemical I Ching: 64 Keys to the Secret of Internal Transformation*

   Vol. 8. *intrachange: I Ching Chess*

SELF-REALIZATION PRACTICES:

   The Five Emanations: Aligning the Modern Mind with the Ancient Soul

   The Spiritual Basis of Good Fortune: Retracing the Ancient Path of Personal Transformation

   Facing Light: Preparing for the Moment of Dying

POETRY:

   Palimpsest Flesh

   Fragments of Anamnesia

   The Soul of Power: Deconstructing the Art of War

   The Tao of Cool: Deconstructing the Tao Te Ching

Made in the USA
San Bernardino, CA
08 January 2020